Tourism, Conflict and Contested Heritage in Former Yugoslavia

Described as 'cultural crossroads' or 'mosaic', 'powder keg', 'border', 'bridge' or Europe's 'Other', the region comprising former Yugoslavia has, over time, conjured up ambiguous imaginaries associated with political unrest, national contest and ethnic divide. Since the disintegration of Yugoslavia and the succeeding Yugoslav Wars of the 1990s, both the geography and historiography of the region have been thoroughly reconfigured, which has impacted the ways in which heritage is interpreted and used at local, regional and national levels. In this ongoing process of heritage (re)interpretation, tourism is more than just a 'dark' spectacle. While it can be seen as a catalyst through which to filter or normalise dissonant memories, it can also be utilised as a powerful ideological tool which enables the narrative reinvention of contested traditions and divisive myths.

Drawing on case studies from Bosnia-Herzegovina, Croatia and Kosovo, this volume generates new and fascinating insights into the contested terrain of heritage tourism in former Yugoslavia. It explores the manifold ways in which tourism stakeholders engage with, capitalise on, and make sense of sites and events marked by conflict and trauma. Unlike many previous studies, this book features contributions by emerging, early-career scholars emanating from within the region, and working across disciplines such as anthropology, art history, geography and political studies.

This book was originally published as a special issue of the *Journal of Tourism and Cultural Change*.

Josef Ploner is a Lecturer at the Faculty of Arts, Cultures and Education at the University of Hull, UK. Trained as a cultural anthropologist, his research focuses on cultural and heritage tourism as sites of learning, ideological contest, narrative ordering and memory formation. Josef's other main research interest relates to mobility, migration and cultural diversity in international higher education.

Patrick Naef is a Researcher and Lecturer in the Department of Geography and Environment at the University of Geneva, Switzerland. He was previously a visiting scholar in the Department of Anthropology at the University of California, Berkeley. His doctoral dissertation defended at the University of Geneva looks at conflicts of memory within the cultural heritage management and tourism sectors in Sarajevo, Srebrenica (Bosnia-Herzegovina) and Vukovar (Croatia). His research in Eastern Europe, South America and South-East Asia has led him to examine notions such as identity, tourism, war, genocide, nationalism and representation.

Tourism, Conflict and Contested Heritage in Former Yugoslavia

Edited by
Josef Ploner and Patrick Naef

LONDON AND NEW YORK

First published 2018 by Routledge

2 Park Square, Milton Park, Abingdon, Oxfordshire OX14 4RN
52 Vanderbilt Avenue, New York, NY 10017

Routledge is an imprint of the Taylor & Francis Group, an informa business

First issued in paperback 2019

British Library Cataloguing in Publication Data
A catalogue record for this book is available from the British Library

ISBN 13: 978-1-138-74451-6 (hbk)
ISBN 13: 978-0-367-23397-6 (pbk)

Typeset in Myriad Pro
by RefineCatch Limited, Bungay, Suffolk

Publisher's Note
The publisher accepts responsibility for any inconsistencies that may have
arisen during the conversion of this book from journal articles to book chapters,
namely the possible inclusion of journal terminology.

Disclaimer
Every effort has been made to contact copyright holders for their permission to
reprint material in this book. The publishers would be grateful to hear from any
copyright holder who is not here acknowledged and will undertake to rectify
any errors or omissions in future editions of this book.

Contents

Citation Information

The chapters in this book were originally published in the *Journal of Tourism and Cultural Change*, volume 14, issue 3 (September 2016). When citing this material, please use the original page numbering for each article, as follows:

Chapter 1
Introduction: Tourism, conflict and contested heritage in former Yugoslavia
Patrick Naef and Josef Ploner
Journal of Tourism and Cultural Change, volume 14, issue 3 (September 2016), pp. 181–188

Chapter 2
Dissonant heritage and promotion of tourism in the case of Serbian medieval monuments in Kosovo
Jelena Pavličić
Journal of Tourism and Cultural Change, volume 14, issue 3 (September 2016), pp. 189–205

Chapter 3
Second World War monuments in Yugoslavia as witnesses of the past and the future
Vladana Putnik
Journal of Tourism and Cultural Change, volume 14, issue 3 (September 2016), pp. 206–221

Chapter 4
Tourism and the 'martyred city': memorializing war in the former Yugoslavia
Patrick Naef
Journal of Tourism and Cultural Change, volume 14, issue 3 (September 2016), pp. 222–239

Chapter 5
Cross-community tourism in Bosnia and Herzegovina: a path to reconciliation?
Emilie Aussems
Journal of Tourism and Cultural Change, volume 14, issue 3 (September 2016), pp. 240–254

Chapter 6
Dark heritage tourism and the Sarajevo siege
Marija Kamber, Theofanis Karafotias and Theodora Tsitoura
Journal of Tourism and Cultural Change, volume 14, issue 3 (September 2016), pp. 255–269

Chapter 7
Memorial policies and restoration of Croatian tourism two decades after the war in former Yugoslavia
Fanny Arnaud
Journal of Tourism and Cultural Change, volume 14, issue 3 (September 2016), pp. 270–290

For any permission-related enquiries please visit:
http://www.tandfonline.com/page/help/permissions

Notes on Contributors

Fanny Arnaud is a graduate student at the Ecole des Hautes Etudes en Sciences Sociales (EHESS) and at the Institut des Sciences sociales du Politique (ISP), Paris, France.

Emilie Aussems is a graduate student at the Institut de sciences politiques Louvian-Europe (ISPOLE), Université Catholique de Louvain (UCLouvain), Louvain-la-Neuve, Belgium. Her research interests include the Balkans, transformations of conflicts, and the role of art and culture in reconciliation.

Marija Kamber is a graduate student of Heritage Management at the University of Kent, Canterbury, UK, and at Athens University of Economics and Business, Athens, Greece. She specialises in cross-cultural communication and the interpretation of conflicting and socio-culturally sensitive topics and in the Dark Heritage sites.

Theofanis Karafotias is a member of the Hellenic Ministry of Culture, Directorate of Conservation of Ancient and Modern Monuments, Athens, Greece.

Patrick Naef is a Researcher and Lecturer at the Department of Geography and Environment, University of Geneva, Switzerland. His doctoral dissertation defended at the University of Geneva looks at conflicts of memory within the cultural heritage management and tourism sectors in Sarajevo, Srebrenica (Bosnia-Herzegovina) and Vukovar (Croatia). His research in Eastern Europe, South America and South-East Asia has led him to examine notions such as identity, tourism, war, genocide, nationalism and representation.

Jelena Pavličić is a Researcher and graduate student of Museology and Heritage Studies at the Faculty of Philosophy, University of Belgrade, Serbia. Her main research interests include the theory and methodology of history of art, theory of museology and heritage axiology.

Josef Ploner is a Lecturer at the Faculty of Arts, Cultures and Education, University of Hull, UK. Trained as a cultural anthropologist, his research focuses on cultural and heritage tourism as sites of learning, ideological contest, narrative ordering and memory formation. Josef's other main research interest relates to mobility, migration and cultural diversity in international higher education.

Vladana Putnik is a Research Associate at the Art History Department, Faculty of Philosophy, University of Belgrade, Serbia. Her field of research is the history of architecture in Serbia and former Yugoslavia in the twentieth century.

Theodora Tsitoura is a graduate student of Heritage Management at the University of Kent, Canterbury, UK, and at Athens University of Economics and Business, Athens, Greece. Her master's field of study was placed in Bosnia-Herzegovina, and it was concerned with the Sarajevo 92–95 war dark heritage, management, tourism and interpretation issues.

Tourism, conflict and contested heritage in former Yugoslavia

Patrick Naef[a] and Josef Ploner[b]

[a]Department of Geography and Environment, University of Geneva, Geneva, Switzerland;
[b]Faculty of Arts, Cultures and Education, University of Hull, Hull, UK

Although, historically, there have always been travellers crossing the Balkan Peninsula, Todorova (1994) notes that early travellers were usually heading for important centres such as Constantinople or Jerusalem, and considered South-East Europe as a peripheral place where people were just passing through. The region is only really discovered in the eighteenth century along with an increasing interest in the East. More organised forms of tourism appear at the beginning of the nineteenth century, emerging first around railway lines and thermal therapy resources, and then expanding towards the coastlines. A large part of these developments took place in Croatia and the 'Dalmatian Riviera', but other regions also experienced the arrival of visitors and the first organised trip in Bosnia was proposed by *Thomas Cook & Sons* in 1898.

It is only after the Second World War, during the rule of Marshall Tito, that tourism really flourished particularly in the period between the 1960s and the 1980s, when the Socialist Federal Republic of Yugoslavia (SFRY) followed an alternative way of development as the rest of the Eastern Bloc. A relative openness to the West allowed the arrival of European tourists and led to forms of mass tourism in some parts of the region (Grandits & Taylor, 2010). While communist regimes such as Bulgaria and Romania mainly hosted eastern 'apparatchiks' on the Black Sea resorts, Yugoslavia and Greece focused on attracting seaside tourists from Western Europe (Cattaruzza & Sintès, 2012).

Tourism and war in the former Yugoslavia

The wars of the Yugoslav succession during the 1990s had, without any doubt, a disastrous impact on the region's tourism sector. Moreover, some of the most popular tourist destinations were directly targeted; the shelling of Dubrovnik, a UNESCO world heritage site on the south coast of Croatia, in 1991 is certainly a paradigmatic example. Bosnia–Herzegovina, Croatia, Kosovo and many other parts of former Yugoslavia were heavily impacted by different armed conflicts and saw tourist numbers plummeting especially during 1992–1995. While Bosnia–Herzegovina was completely ravaged and saw its tourism brought to a complete halt, some regions of Croatia were spared and tourism did not vanish entirely. Since the end of the wars, the revival of tourism has unfolded in contrasting and asynchronous ways. Countries such as Croatia and Slovenia quickly regained the number of tourists they had before the conflicts, but Bosnia–Herzegovina attained its pre-war tourism market only a few years ago (a market far smaller than its Croatian neighbour).

Nowadays, Croatia, and above all its coastline, certainly represents the epicentre of tourism in the former Yugoslavia and some consider seaside tourism as 'hegemonic' in the region (Pinteau, 2011). Other former republics of Yugoslavia are also profiting from tourism. For example, Montenegro promotes its coastline to eastern European tourists – mainly Serbians and Russians – and to a lesser extent to the West. Natural attractions represent the main assets of the non-coastal countries, while the cultural heritage of this region, often described as a 'crossroads between East and West' (Bracewell & Drace-Francis, 2009), constitutes another important touristic resource. In this context, Serbia, Kosovo and Bosnia–Herzegovina promote their religious heritage extensively; their numerous mosques and Roman Catholic or Orthodox churches, some of them designated as world heritage sites by UNESCO, constitute important landmarks on the tourism map.

Paradoxically, the wars of the 1990s also contributed to the cultural heritage production in the former Yugoslavia, leading to the touristification of the war memory – a phenomenon sometimes also referred to as 'war tourism' – through the construction of war memorials and museums, along with the organisation of 'war tours' (Naef, 2014). This trend, which draws on both domestic and international tourism markets, is especially present in heavily war-torn places like Sarajevo, the capital of Bosnia–Herzegovina, and Slavonia, a region in Eastern Croatia.

In Sarajevo, war is now part of the tourism offer, and besides several museums on the topic, some local tour operators offer tailored tours focusing on the remains of the last war. Elsewhere, the Memorial of Srebrenica-Potočari receives more than 100,000 annual visitors, mourners as well as tourists each year, making it one of the most visited sites of Bosnia–Herzegovina today (Naef, 2014). In both contexts, tourism participates in memory conflicts, in a country ruled by three different communities (Bosnians, Croats and Serbs) previously opposed (and sometimes allied) in warfare.

The Croatian region of Slavonia, and especially the town of Vukovar, often heralded as a symbol of both national martyrdom and independence, also experience a form of memorial tourism, in which Croats from all over the country come to pay their respects to this martyred town and region (Naef, 2016). From a tourism and destination planning perspective, the interpretation of the conflict is unilateral. Memorial politics, predominantly in the hands of Croatian war veterans, serve as a base for the diffusion of a hegemonic discourse on the past war. Furthermore, the symbol of independence associated with Vukovar is often used in nationalistic narratives, in politics and the media, as well as in museums and tourism. Although Vukovar is the focus of tourism associated with war heritage, Croatian tourism authorities have been very active in distancing the rest of the country from its war-torn image. Rivera (2008) speaks about an 'omission' of war, a process that she qualifies as 'covering'. Croatian tourism politics seeks to dissociate the country from its war heritage, but also tries to promote Croatia as 'European', emphasising Roman or Austro-Hungarian historical elements, instead of Byzantine, socialist or Slavic culture (Rivera, 2008).

In their touristscapes and memorialscapes (Carr, 2012), where competing memories are at stake, these new countries, and places within them, make different uses of the past. Exploring the management of tourism is thus essential to the comprehension of memorial issues in the former Yugoslavia. Besides, considering the importance of history (and of its instrumentalisation) in the region, an analysis of the impact of memory on tourism seems even more necessary. Since the 1980s, tourism has been identified as a potential instrument of peace by international bodies such as UNESCO, UNWTO or the European Commission. However, as it can be observed in parts of ex-Yugoslavia, tourism can also contribute to increasing memorial tensions.

Contested memories and dissonant heritage in tourism

The mutual and arguably complex relationships between tourism, memory and heritages of war and conflict have been widely explored in tourism studies and generated a wealth of international case studies. These include tourisms associated with the American Civil War (Chronis, 2012), the First and Second World Wars (Cooper, 2006; Scates, 2006; Winter, 2012), Vietnam (Henderson, 2000), Cambodia (Sion, 2011), Rwanda (Friedrich & Johnston, 2013), Sri Lanka (Hyndman & Amarasingam, 2014), Bosnia and Herzegovina (Causevic & Lynch, 2011; Naef, 2014), the Middle East (Milstein, 2013), as well as tours to more recent sites of terrorism (Sather-Wagstaff, 2011). Likewise, authors have developed a wide range of concepts and heuristic 'labels' to make sense of tourism practices and representations within potentially contested moral and memorial terrain, such as 'dark' or 'thanatourism' (Foley & Lennon, 1996; Seaton, 1999; Stone, 2006), 'battlefield tourism' (Dunkley, Morgan, & Westwood, 2011; Ryan, 2007), '(post-)war' or 'post-conflict tourism', 'atrocity heritage' (Ashworth, 2004; Fyall, Prideaux, & Timothy, 2006), or alternatively, 'Phoenix tourism' (Causevic & Lynch, 2011), 'reconciliation tourism' (Higgins-Desbiolles, 2003) as well as 'peace tourism' (Moufakkir & Kelly, 2010). The variety of concepts currently in use seems to point towards a certain (moral?) dilemma within tourism studies, which suggests a threefold pattern in the interpretation of sites of war and terror. Firstly, these sites are conceptualised as marketable destinations capitalising on tourists' peculiar and sometimes voyeuristic fascination with the 'dark' and uncanny dimensions of the human condition. Secondly, they are seen as material and emotional sites of personal and collective remembrance (e.g. ancestral/battlefield tourism). And finally, they are approached as arenas in which lasting hostilities and traumas can be overcome and 'normalised' with the help of tourism (e.g. tourism for peace, regenerative tourism, etc.).

In an influential study, Tunbridge and Ashworth (1996) highlighted the significance of site management and interpretation in relation to what they termed 'dissonant heritage'. Such heritage is appropriated by different and conflicting groups of stakeholders, including victims or descendants of victims, perpetrators and their descendants, bystanders as well as other groups including tourists, refugees and displaced persons, international NGOs or heritage organisations. Clearly, tourism plays an important part in the interpretation and management of such dissonant heritage and scholars have repeatedly emphasised the ideological influence of tourism in the brokerage of memory and its power to utilise narratives that direct audiences towards certain attitudes and moral judgements (Bendix, 2002; Ploner, 2012). For the region comprising former Yugoslavia, this may relate to well-rehearsed grand narratives mapping out a distinct orientalist Balkan identity (i.e. *Balkanism*, see Todorova, 1997; or *Balkan atavism*, see Herzfeld, 2005), as well as more punctuated recent (hi)stories about war, death and survival (see Naef and Aussems, this issue). For example, Dragićević Šešić and Rogač Mijatović (2014) describe how tourism and contemporary forms of heritage interpretation reinforce long-established narratives and symbolic geographies of the Balkan region within Europe through politically charged metaphors such as 'multicultural mosaic', 'bridge', 'border', 'crossroads', 'powder keg' or Europe's

'Other'. At a different and more local level, Causevic and Lynch (2011) have demonstrated how individuals such as tour guides in Sarajevo and Mostar negotiate dissonant memories by escaping everyday politicking and by engaging in an empathic personal narrative 'catharsis'. Such catharsis emerges from the interaction between tour guide, site and tourist and seeks to present a message of peace going beyond the dominant political discourse and the 'banalism' often associated with heritage interpretation in tourism.

Between these local and the greater regional 'Balkan' narratives, the renegotiation and reinvention of collective memory and heritage through tourism remains particularly problematic at national levels. Following the wars of the Yugoslav succession and the emergence of six independent states on former Yugoslav territory in the 1990s, tourism has not only been identified as a tool for post-war economic recovery, but has also been instrumental in the politically motivated reinvention of tradition, the annulment of recent history, and attempts to reorganise national collective memory and structures of feeling. In this context, tourism has been harnessed as a strategic tool within wider national politics of collective amnesia rather than an agent of memory and reconciliation. Considering research evidence to date, this has been particularly the case in Croatia, which has arguably profited most from international tourism since the late 1990s, but continues to conceal and remove any material and narrative traces reminiscent of the recent war (Arnauld, 2016; Rivera, 2008).

The narrative power of tourism in inventing, adapting and obliterating dissonant national historiographies is well recorded in the literature (Pitchford, 2008; Ploner, 2012) and seems particularly momentous in post-war scenarios where myths and nostalgic references to more remote, and hence less problematic pasts are frequently reinvigorated (Boym, 2001). However, as Pavlicic (2016) shows, medieval sites such as Serbian churches and monasteries in Kosovo are not spared from ongoing ideological battles over heritage interpretation and ownership claims which are inextricably linked to more recent and lived memories of conflict. While Lennon and Foley's (2000) claim that more recent events are generally 'darker' than those with a longer history may be valid, one has also to acknowledge the symbolic potential of historically remote sites and events in refuelling ongoing political, religious or ethnic tensions.

Deconstructing such ideological and conflicting symbolisms imbued in monuments and heritage sites is a common theme within critical heritage and tourism studies and, to some extent, features in this special issue. However, as Boym (2011) argues with reference to Walter Benjamin, memory cannot be reduced to the symbolic realm alone, but is more akin to 'allegorical' ways of interpreting, thinking and feeling. Writing about ruins – more often seen as allegories of romantic nostalgia rather than post-war memorialscapes – Boym makes strong claims for a memory in appreciation of ruins ('ruinophilia') which is less retrospective and restorative of imaginary pasts, but offers prospective views towards '(…) possible futures that never came to be' (Boym, 2011, no pagination). Following this reading, the papers presented in this special issue do not only look backward but also point in the direction of utopian and 'nostalgic futures' by highlighting the potential for reconciliation and peace.

Authors' contributions

Much has been written in the last 20 years about the atrocious wars in the former Yugoslavia. Tourism, however, remains a largely understudied field, particularly in those Yugoslav succession states which have less profited from international tourist arrivals than others. Furthermore, a paternalist and somewhat condescending attitude toward the region, with the voice of international experts and scholars tending to silence the local discourses, is often criticised (Todorova, 1997; Tumarkin, 2005). This edition of the *Journal of Tourism and Cultural Change* aims to address some of these shortcomings. It is purposefully presented as a 'young scholars' issue since the majority of contributors are young/early-career researchers who emanate from the region and, at best, have vague childhood memories of the events that took place during the early 1990s. The criticality, reflexivity, and often bold argumentation brought forward by these emerging 'post-war' scholars, add fresh perspectives to the study of tourism in post-conflict settings and equally emphasises the significance of tourism as a key agent for social and cultural change. The authors featured in this collection also draw on a wealth of existing regional and other non-Anglophone scholarship which, so far, has been widely ignored in the mainstream literature and adds more nuanced perspectives to this field of study.

If tourism constitutes the central theme of these articles, all the scholars featured here explore fields going beyond the scope of tourism alone such as art, politics, NGOs, religious heritage, to mention only a few. Likewise, tourism sectors and practices are set in different political and cultural contexts, and their study can reveal tensions, struggles and potentialities expanding far beyond this industry alone. An interdisciplinary perspective therefore guides this collection of articles contributed by scholars from disciplines as diverse as political sciences, anthropology, art history, museology and geography, and analysing case studies that encompass Kosovo, Bosnia–Herzegovina and Croatia.

Although touristic forms of heritage promotion and interpretation in former Yugoslavia often result in complex amalgamations of historically detached sites and events, the papers in this issue follow a 'historical' or chronological order.

In the first paper, Jelena Pavlicic, a museologist from Pristina, explores how medieval religious Serbian heritage sites in Kosovo have been gradually rendered inaccessible and neglected by Kosovan–Albanian elites who use heritage tourism as a tool for building a new national identity. Reflecting on both Central European and Anglophone scholarly traditions in museology and heritage interpretation, and drawing on a range of empirical materials (i. e. ethnographic observations, tourist brochures and website narratives), the author diagnoses a latent 'physical and semantic iconoclasm' which, paradoxically, emphasises the monuments' regional and international symbolic value (e.g. as endangered UNESCO world heritage sites). Calling for an 'active policy of memory', Pavlicic poses important questions about the ambivalent role of tourism – either as an arena for integrative and sustainable heritage management, or conversely, as an instrument assisting modern iconoclasm.

In the second paper, University of Belgrade-based art historian Vladana Putnik revisits the Second World War Monuments erected in Yugoslavia between the 1960s and the 1980s. Commemorating partisan and civilian martyrdom, and embodying an expressive modernist aesthetic, these often gargantuan structures were popular sites for political pilgrimages and educational tourism celebrating national unity and forging collective history within Tito's socialist state. Considered as reminders of an unwanted past after the breakup of Yugoslavia, many of these monuments were neglected, forgotten and left to decay, but more recently, have also drawn a new clientele of tourists in the wake of 'Yugo-nostalgia' and through the bohemian appreciation by international artists, film-makers and photographers. In this study, Putnik guides the reader through a tumultuous history of heritage (re-)interpretation, and poses the interesting question whether the monuments' artistic value can eventually outstrip ideological narrative and political calcu-lus. In her text, tourism is identified as a powerful means for education and revitalisation which could lead to more 'objective' and dialogic forms of heritage interpretation.

The following article by Guest-Editor Patrick Naef explores the notion of the 'martyred city', a recurrent memorial designation associated with war-torn cities such as Berlin, Guer-nica, Hiroshima, Homs and many more. However, rather than dwelling on popular and quasi-religious media discourses of martyrdom, Naef proposes 'martyred city' as a concep-tual frame through which to approach the ambivalent ways in which different 'memorial entrepreneurs' negotiate the blurred boundaries between martyrdom and victimhood in the cities of Vukovar (Croatia) and Sarajevo (Bosnia–Herzegovina). By inspecting the dynamic post-war geographies of these two cities, Naef maps out contested 'memorials-capes' of martyrdom/victimhood which are marked and animated by everyday (touristic) practices and events such as guided tours, museum exhibitions, film festivals, posters and graffiti. However, while the 'martyred city' may be tributary to the everyday (and often creative) sociocultural organisation of place, the progressing 'touristification' and 'heritagi-sation' can also mean 'freezing' a place around a particular historical event.

Emilie Aussems' paper 'Cross-community tourism in Bosnia and Herzegovina – a path to reconciliation'? looks at the challenging work of two NGOs, which organise tours to civil and military memorials for former soldiers and other members of the Serbian, Croat and Muslim communities in Bosnia and Herzegovina. Identifying four dimensions of reconcilia-tion-through-tourism (economic, educational, therapeutic and leisure), Aussems presents some powerful narratives of tour participants which range between grief, denial, guilt, empathy and catharsis. While these cross-community tours represent an overall positive bottom-up approach to post-war reconciliation processes, the author also refers to wider contextual and societal issues impacting on the success or failure of these tours such as the lack of trust, the varying symbolic connotations of memorial sites, as well as the risk of volunteers and tour participants being exposed to pressures coming from poli-ticians and members within their own (ethnic, national or religious) communities.

Important questions about the management of dissonant heritage sites are also addressed in the paper by Kamber, Karafotias and Tsitoura: 'Dark Heritage Tourism and the Sarajevo Siege'. Drawing on the concept of 'dark heritage', and presenting findings from a survey conducted with tourists visiting the so-called Tunnel of Hope (Sarajevo's life-line during the siege years 1992–1995), the authors identify a range of motivations of tour-ists visiting the sites as well as experiences gained during their visits. Among other interesting insights, the findings suggest that the 'Tunnel of Hope' tour particularly appeals to young and well-educated Western tourists who seek to establish 'authentic' and 'tangible' connections to the everyday struggles for survival in the besieged city, but are also driven by curiosity and educational motivations. The authors conclude that, while the 'Tunnel of Hope' represents an overall well-managed 'alternative' heritage site, more far-reaching national tourism and heritage policies contributing to social renewal and reconciliation still remain widely underdeveloped.

The final paper in this special issue is presented by Fanny Arnauld and is based on her Ph.D. research on tourism and memory formation in Croatia. Critically analysing current tourism marketing strategies in Croatia, Arnauld shows how national elites and tourism policy-makers continue to hide away contested war memories under a glossy surface of unspoilt natural beauty, historically remote heritage, as well as an idyllic imagery of sun, sand and sea. While Croatia's active role in the war of the 1990s is ideologically redressed in narratives of victimhood and defence against aggressive neighbours, current tourism representations follow (and support) a wider strategy of 'de-Balkanisation' in that the country is internationally refashioned as a 'novel' holiday option on par with, yet distinct from, well-established Mediterranean destinations. Challenging this national reinvention of tradition through tourism, Arnauld calls for more active and engaged national policies of memory which reach out to both local and international publics.

Although this special issue addresses a broad range of critical issues gravitating around the interpretation of heritage and memory in post-Yugoslavian tourism contexts, there is much scope for future research in this field. For example, scholars could look more closely at national case studies in tourism development, heritage discourses and policies which, for various reasons, have received fairly modest attention in academic writing, such as Serbia, Montenegro and to some extent, Macedonia and Slovenia. Likewise, scholars interested in reconciliatory and pro-peace forms of tourism, could engage more vigorously in longitudinal projects exploring the success or failure of different initiatives at local, regional, national and international levels.

The special issue presented here is strong proof that, some twenty years after the end of the wars in Yugoslavia, an emerging generation of interdisciplinary international researchers continue to challenge one-dimensional heritage formations and interpretations, and try to make sense of unwanted, repressed or otherwise contested pasts. While tourism is but one element in these complex processes of meaning-making, it is also a valuable conceptual and empirical frame through which to gain insight into the multifaceted practices and politics of memory and forgetting.

References

Ashworth, G. J. (2004). Tourism and the heritage of atrocity: Managing the heritage of South African apartheid for entertainment. In T. V. Singh (ed.), *New horizons in tourism* (pp. 95–108). Basingstoke: CABI.

Bendix, R. (2002). Capitalizing on memories past, present, and future: Observations on the intertwining of tourism and narration. *Anthropological Theory*, 2(4), 469–487.

Boym, S. (2001). *The future of nostalgia*. New York, NY: Basic Books.

Boym, S. (2011). Ruinophilia: Appreciation of Ruins. In *Atlas of transformation* (online). Retrieved March 25, 2016, from http://monumenttotransformation.org/atlas-of-transformation/html/r/ruinophilia/ruinophilia-appreciation-of-ruins-svetlana-boym.html

Bracewell, W., & Drace-Francis, A. (2009). *Balkan departures: Travel writing from Southeastern Europe*. New York, NY: Berghahn.

Carr, G. (2012). Examining the memorialscape of occupation and liberation: A case study from the Channel Islands. *International Journal of Heritage Studies*, 18(2), 174–193.

Cattaruzza, A., & Sintès, P. (2012). *Atlas géopolitique des Balkans. Un autre visage de l'Europe*. Paris: Autrement.

Causevic, S., & Lynch, P. (2011). Phoenix tourism. Post-conflict tourism role. *Annals of Tourism Research*, 38(3), 780–800.

Chronis, A. (2012). Between place and story: Gettysburg as tourism imagery. *Annals of Tourism Research*, 39(4), 1797–1816.

Cooper, M. (2006). The pacific war battlefields: Tourist attraction or war memorials? *International Journal of Tourism Research*, 8(3), 213–222.

Dragićević Šešić, M., Rogač Mijatović, L. (2013). Balkan dissonant heritage narratives (and their attractiveness) for tourism. *American Journal of Tourism Management*, 3(1B), 10–19.

Dunkley, R., Morgan, N., & Westwood, S. (2011). Visiting the trenches: Exploring meanings and motivations in battlefield tourism. *Tourism Management, 32*(4), 860–868.

Arnauld, F. (2016). Memorial policies and restoration of Croatian tourism two decades after the war in former Yugoslavia. *Journal of Tourism and Cultural Change.* doi:10.1080/14766825.2016.1169348

Foley, M., & Lennon, J. (1996). JFK and dark tourism: A fascination with assassination. *International Journal of Heritage Studies, 2*(4), 198–211.

Friedrich, M., & Johnston, T. (2013). Beauty versus tragedy: Thanatourism and the memorialisation of the 1994 Rwandan genocide. *Journal of Tourism and Cultural Change, 11*(4), 302–320.

Fyall, A., Prideaux, B., & Timothy, D. (2006). War and tourism: An introduction. *International Journal of Tourism Research, 8*(3), 153–155.

Grandits, H., & Taylor, K. (Eds.). (2010). *Yugoslavia's sunny side: A history of tourism and socialism (1950s–1980s)*. Budapest: CEU Press.

Henderson, J. C. (2000). War as a tourist attraction: The case of Vietnam. *International. Journal of Tourism Research, 2*(1), 269–280.

Herzfeld, M. (2005). *Cultural intimacy. Social poetics in the nation-state*. Abingdon: Routledge.

Higgins-Desbiolles, F. (2003). Reconciliation tourism: Tourism healing divided societies? *Tourism Recreation Research, 28*(3), 35–44.

Hyndman, J. N., & Amarasingam, A. (2014). Touring 'Terrorism': Landscapes of memory in post-war Sri Lanka. *Geography Compass, 8*(8), 560–575.

Lennon, J., & Foley, M. (2000). *Dark tourism – The attraction of death and disaster*. London: Continuum.

Milstein, T. (2013). Communicating 'normalcy' in Israel: Intra/intercultural paradox and interpretations in tourism discourse. *Journal of Tourism and Cultural Change, 11*(1–2), 73–91.

Moufakkir, O., & Kelly, I. (2010). *Tourism, progress and peace*. Wallingford: CABI.

Naef, P. (2014). *Guerre, tourisme et mémoire dans l'espace post-yougoslave: la construction de la 'ville-martyre'*(Doctoral dissertation). Geneva: University of Geneva.

Naef, P. (2016). Tourism and the 'martyred city': Memorializing war in the former Yugoslavia. *Journal of Tourism and Cultural Change.* doi: 10.1080/14766825.2016.1169345

Pavličić, J. (2016). Dissonant heritage and promotion of tourism in the case of Serbian medieval monuments in Kosovo. *Journal of Tourism and Cultural Change.* doi:10.1080/14766825.2016.1169349

Pinteau. (2011). *Le tourisme en Croatie. De la création d'une image touristique à son instrumentalisation* (Doctoral dissertation). Clermont-Ferrand: University Blaise Pascal.

Pitchford, S. (2008). *Identity tourism: Imaging and imagining the nation*. Bingley: Emerald.

Ploner, J. (2012). Tourist literature and the ideological grammar of landscape in the Austrian Danube Valley, ca. 1870–1945. *Journal of Tourism History, 4*(3), 237–257.

Rivera, L. (2008). Managing 'spoiled' national identity: War, tourism, and memory in Croatia. *American Sociological Review, 73*, 613–34.

Ryan, C. (Ed.). (2007). *Battlefield tourism: History, place and interpretation*. Amsterdam: Elsevier.

Sather-Wagstaff, J. (2011). *Heritage that hurts: Tourists in the memoryscapes of September 11*. Walnut Creek: Left Coast Press.

Scates, B. (2006). *Return to Gallipoli: Walking the battlefields of the Great War*. Melbourne: Melbourne University Press.

Seaton, A. V. (1999). War and thanatourism: Waterloo 1815–1914. *Annals of Tourism Research, 37*(4), 130–158.

Sion, B. (2011). Conflicting sites of memory in post-genocide Cambodia. *Humanity, 2*(1), 1–21.

Stone, P. (2006). A dark tourism spectrum: Towards a typology of death and macabre related tourist sites, attractions and exhibitions. *TOURISM: An Interdisciplinary International Journal, 54*(2), 145–160.

Todorova, M. (1994). The Balkans: From discovery to invention. *Slavic Review, 53*, 453–482.

Todorova, M. (1997). *Imagining the Balkans*. Oxford: Oxford University Press.

Tumarkin, M. (2005). *Traumascapes: The power and fate of places transformed by tragedy*. Melbourne: Melbourne University Press.

Tunbridge, J. E., & Ashworth, G. J. (1996). *Dissonant heritage: The management of the past as a resource in conflict*. Chichester: John Wiley.

Winter, C. (2012). Commemorating the Great War on the Somme: Exploring personal connections. *Journal of Tourism and Cultural Change, 10*(3), 248–263.

Dissonant heritage and promotion of tourism in the case of Serbian medieval monuments in Kosovo

Jelena Pavličić[a,b]

[a]Faculty of Arts, University of Pristina, Kosovska Mitrovica, Serbia; [b]Center for Museology and Heritology, Belgrade, Serbia

ABSTRACT

During and after the war in Kosovo in 1999, Serbian medieval monuments were recognised as symbols and bearers of Serbian identity. This led to the fact that among the Albanian population in Kosovo, they were seen as an undesirable legacy – a reflection of centuries of the existence of Serbs in Kosovo. Although the historical value of these monuments, four of which are on the UNESCO World Heritage list of endangered sites, is not disputed, popular tourist publications open an unfounded debate and are used to alienate the historical identity of these places or to promote a distorted interpretation of them. Through popular media representations this paper will touch on the complexity of these monuments as dissonant heritage in the newly established state of Kosovo and its different uses and interpretations in the promotion of tourism.

Introduction

As a consequence of the wars and subsequent socio-political changes in the Balkans, the interpretations of the past remain a contested issue. Significant parts of the heritage became 'dissonant heritage', which according to Tunbridge and Ashworth (1996, p. 27) is related to the process of coping with ambivalent and largely unwanted pasts. The problem of interpretation and promotion of heritage is difficult due to various economic and political factors. Not only what is interpreted, but how and by whom it is interpreted, is creating specific messages about the value and the meaning of specific heritage sites and the past they represent.

After the war in Kosovo in 1999, the other type of war began and is still being fought, implying the destruction of the Serbian cultural artefacts as a means of dominating the enemy (Bevan, 2006, p. 8). This heritage – selected and interpreted as the 'heritage of others' – saw different types of treatment it was used, neglected and interpreted in many ways, especially during the war and later in the transition period in the region. Within this politics of creating a distinct national identity of the new Kosovan nation-state, the heritage from earlier periods was incorporated or rejected as a 'threat to the national cultural identity' (Šešić Dragićević & Rogač Mijatović, 2014, p. 12).

As heritage itself is not a relic of the past but a potential for sustainable development of communities (Faro convention, 2005) it is very often explored and exploited through tourism. Tourism is a phenomenon of great importance in the globalising world – not only because it is in accordance with the patterns of the global economy, but also because it produces an interest in specific experiences, artefacts and local narratives (Šešić Dragićević, 2011, pp. 14–37). It could empower people, but also be used in consti-tuting targeted 'communities' by the imagined or real narrative (Salazar, 2012, p. 9).

This research paper acknowledges the significance of social and cultural development of Serbia, the region of Kosovo and Metohija, as well as the whole Balkan region, which requires to critically discuss the conflicting interpretations of heritage occurring in this region today. It is essential to approach heritage with all its contradictions and complex-ities in order to make it an important asset in the development of tourism and, above all, of a cohesive society. According to this, understanding the ways in which heritage is 'used' (Smith, 2006) in Kosovo is the first step towards a potential solution of the problem in line with contemporary understanding of the idea of heritage and its treatment in theory and practice.

The focus of this paper is on four heritage sites designated as 'Medieval Monuments in Kosovo'[1], which represent Serbia on the UNESCO World Heritage List. Since there are dif-ficulties in monitoring and managing these sites due to the post-conflict political instabil-ity in the region, they are inscribed as 'under threat' by UNESCO (UNESCO, 2006). On the one hand, these monuments were included in the 'World Heritage in Danger' list as an unwanted heritage in contemporary Kosovo society, while, on the other hand, the list made them worthy of remembrance in this young pro-European state. Such characteris-ation turns these monuments into representative examples of dissonant heritage in Kosovo and Metohija and their contemporary use and actualisation in tourism raise a ques-tion about the real danger of this heritage.

This paper draws attention to how selected heritage sites are being interpreted for tour-ists across various media.

The empirical data for this article were collected during short visits made in the period between 2008 and 2014. The main research method used in the field has been the content analysis of visual and textual information about heritage that is presented in touristic pro-motion of the sites. It is recognised as a transmitter of certain messages interpreted here in accordance with contributions of the modern discipline of Memory culture, new theories in Museology and the General Theory of Heritage (named Heritology), which defines theory approach to heritage in the Balkans.

Theorising heritage – regional and international perspectives

Understanding the past as a means for envisioning the future from the present perspective (Kuljić, 2006, p. 30) corresponds with Jan Assman's interpretation of history as 'an expression of certain epoch's requirements and needs and as a cultural construction' (Assman, 2001, p. 65). History, then, is not only about the past, but also about the present, because it actively participates in the creation of everyday reality, people's iden-tity and our vision and comprehension of the world. In such a way, the past is used as a 'wonder' able to explain contemporary events and solve current problems (Kuljić, 2006, p. 214). Cultural heritage as intrinsic part of both past and present seems to keep that aura of the *miraculous*, especially when it comes to religious heritage sites (Chastel, 1986). As opposed to that sacred dimension of heritage, contemporary recognition and evaluation of heritage through heritage organisations is usually done by promoting profane values such as the exclusivity, uniqueness, originality, universality of an object.[2] In this reading, heritage is primarily characterised by its duration and unchangeability, by its ability to display lasting signs of certain antiquity in any given social context or circumstances (Bulatović & Milosavljević, 1999, p. 239).

Nevertheless, in the second half of the twentieth century the idea of heritage and its uses was challenged across academic disciplines. For example, new theories in museology challenged the idea that heritage value is self-evident and introduced new aspects of memory, identity of an object, local community and participants in exploring the value of an object (Mensch, 1992, p. 32; Vergo, 1989, p. 3). The genesis of this theoretical 'extensions' rests upon two approaches: the Anglo-Saxon and Central-European. The first one is based on the foundations of *new museology*, and is advocated by the theorists from the English-speaking world. The focus of their research is more on the museum practice and museography, so a syntagm *museum studies* and *heritage studies* is also in use. The Central-European approach, on the other hand, takes *musealia* as the primary subject of museological research (Mensch, 1992, pp. 41–46; Popadić, 2015, pp. 154–155). Hence, the basic difference is in the subject of research, recognised through relation *object-item* (Bulatović, 2009). In 1970, Czech museologist Zbinek Stransky brings in the concept of *museality* (Stransky, 1970, p. 35) as a characteristic of *musealia* – an object of the material world, which documents the 'reality' of the primary or archaeological context from which it was removed. When applied to the heritage as immovable property in space, this means that buildings and their complexes can document the physical and spiritual context in which they originated and existed, with all the values and meanings they had acquired during the course of their existence (Maroević, 1993, p. 96).

Shortly afterwards, Maroević (1983, 1993) developed an 'information theory' of heritage, according to which the characteristics of museality, that is, the capacity of museality as testimony, are attributed to the entire heritage. This theoretical approach had an important impact on the holistic approach in understanding the idea of heritage in the Balkans and beyond. In 1982, Tomislav Šola, a museologist from Zagreb, proposed a unique scientific discipline, which integrated the already existing ones. It was based on the phenomenon of heritage itself and it was named 'heritology'. This discipline broadens the definition of museology in such a way that it consolidates new museological manifestations and has a holistic approach to the problems of protection and treatment of the entire heritage. In the last two decades, heritology has become a scientific discipline that not only corresponds to the traditional aims of museology, but also aims at understanding the origin and nature of heritage, the purpose of inheritance as well as the forms and potentials of the *uses of heritage* in the contemporary world.

The theme 'uses of heritage', as dominant in any transition period, is more elaborately explored in the book of the same name, by Laurajane Smith, published in 2006. She demonstrated that heritage value was not inherent in physical objects or places, but rather that these objects and places were used to give tangibility to the values that underpin different communities and to assert them. Maroević and Šola, as well as, later on, Serbian museologist Bulatović have theorised about cultural heritage as an experience resulting from social, cultural and individual histories, emphasising its material values as a product of that experience (Bulatović, 2005, 2009; Maroević, 1993, 2004; Šola, 1997, 2014). Mapping the same heritage discourse, Smith presents the idea of an 'authorized heritage discourse' and challenges the traditional 'Western' (!) definitions of heritage that focus on material and monumental forms of 'old', or aesthetically pleasing, tangible heritage. Here, themes such as intangibility, identity, memory and remembering, perform-ance, place, and dissonance are developed and used in various combinations to explore different aspects of the uses of heritage. Smith understands heritage as a cultural process that engages with the acts of remembering that create ways to engage with the present. (Smith, 2006, pp. 3–44). Her position is closely related to the attitudes of the prominent Balkan theorists, who understand heritage as a transmitter of messages and information about different realities in which it originated and developed.

Smith observed that the uses of heritage were consequently often bound up with power relations, and specifically the power to legitimise and de-legitimise cultures (Smith, 2006, p. 81). This is because powerful groups have been actively successful, over time, in defining what does and does not qualify as the nation's heritage. Such hegemonic definitions promote the idea that heritage is about a common national inheritance and it concerns a singular past that must not be tampered with. Nevertheless, such a definition of heritage is focused on the interpretation of heritage in the context of social functions and cultural processes, which are important but not the only contexts for understanding the heritage (Popadić, 2015, p. 33). Smith's study offers the opportunity to better understand contemporary social processes and the role of heritage in them, but not to affirm them as their only meaning.

In interpreting potentially dissonant uses of heritage, we are interested in interpreting the endangered Serbian medieval monuments in Kosovo through the promotion of tourism, it is important to preserve the scientific truth/historical value, despite the chal-lenge of postmodernism with its multitude of narratives. When speaking about the pres-entation of monuments of a rich and complex cultural past, history of conservation underlines the presentation of historical layer which defines the very identity of a certain place (Maroević, 1993, pp. 243–249).

War crisis and a sense of heritage. The case of religious medieval sites in Kosovo and Metohija

As Chastel, a French art historian, (1986) reminds us, war crises awake a new sense of heri-tage and often reveal the true price of it. The war in the Autonomous Region of Kosovo and Metohija in 1999 brings up the question of the fundamental sense and meaning of heritage. Frequently described as a vital cross-roads of cultures in the Balkans, 'every stone' in this region may be referred to as a testimony of the presence of different religions and civilisations throughout history. Still, in the years after the 1999, war in Serbia, in the Autonomous Region of Kosovo and Metohija, cultural heritage was not protected as 'common heritage', in accordance with international legal acts, conventions and stan-dards. On the contrary, it became a repressed and instrumentalised national product of the political situation. By means of the Resolution 1244, adopted by the United Nations Security Council in 1999, a mandate of warrant for the freedom, justice and peace in the Autonomous Region of Kosovo and Metohija was given to the United Nations. Respon-sibility for protection of human lives, freedom and security was thus transferred to the international public authorities, the administration of United Nations Interim Administration Mission in Kosovo (UNMIK), and the international military forces – Kosovo Force (KFOR).[3] Unfortunately, as early as in June 1999 this responsibility was seriously challenged – more than 220,000 Serbs and members of other non-Albanian communities were exiled, while about 120 Christian religious objects and cultural monuments were devastated or destroyed (Jokić, 2003; UNESCO, 2003). The repression was continued, and the last significant eruption of violence of Albanians against Serbs living in the region, was organised and carried out between the 17th and 19th of March 2004. In these destructive assaults, thousands of Albanians, led by armed groups of extremists and members of the Kosovo Protection Corps, carried out the ethnic cleansing, which also included destruction of houses, private property, Orthodox Christian religious sites and cultural monuments (Jokić, 2004, p. 8).[4] If we speak about orthodox medieval churches as cultural monuments, then, this was only the beginning of their 'deliberate suppression' and destruction.

During and after the war in Kosovo in 1999, Serbian medieval monuments were recognised as symbols and bearers of Serbian identity within the region. They extend the Serbian presence into the past and legitimise it in the present and into the future, which is the model that Bevan (2006, p. 8) recognised in many others conflict areas. Although historical facts about these monuments are not disputed, popular publications open an unfounded debate and are used to obliterate the historical identity of these places and to distort interpretation. Among sites on the UNESCO World Heritage in Danger List (inscribed in 2006), and generally titled 'Medieval Monuments in Kosovo' are four Serbian Orthodox edifices and complexes: the Dečani Monastery (included on the World Heritage Site List in 2004), the Patriarchate of Peć Monastery, The Church of the Holy Virgin of Ljeviš (Prizren) and the Gračanica Monastery. They are recognised as a unified group of churches that represent important Byzantine-Romanesque ecclesiastical culture between the thirteenth and seventeenth centuries.[5]

These monuments have not had their own curators since 1999, so tourists could rely only on printed guides, local Albanian tourist guides and, ultimately, the monks. However, due to the inaccessibility of the monuments themselves, printed and internet publications have the primary role in informing tourists. Through them, these monuments are often misinterpreted and used for creating an ideologically desired image of the newly established state and its new, 'pure' identity. This is unsurprising because beside national cultural canons and traditions, cultural tourism recalling the historical significance of the nation is very often used within the process of identity building (Šešić Dragićević & Rogač Mijatović, 2014, p. 14).

'Heritage in everyday life'

One personal story from visiting Prizren in 2013 will be used here as paradigmatic experience, relevant for understanding the contested uses of heritage, here in the case of The Church of the Holy Virgin of Ljeviš in Prizren.

> We are in front of the church of St. Friday, now. Some people say it is from the middle ages, but it has seven stages of development. It was built on the foundations of an Illyrian basilica, and then in the eighteenth century it was the mosque. Now it is the church. I do not know why it's closed, why nobody wants to open the door. Otherwise, this church is on the UNESCO World Heritage in Danger List. I don't know what else to tell you about it. (personal memos from 28.10.2013)

These are the words of an architect, responsible for guiding the participants of the regional seminar 'Past Stories & Future Memories' organised by the Swedish organisation Cultural Heritage without Borders (CHwB) in Prizren, a town in southern Kosovo, in October 2013.[6] The motto of the seminar was summarised in the sentence 'Stories bring places alive and make them relevant to people in contemporary settings, but many stories get buried or lost', so the aim of the meeting was to encourage and educate participants 'to focus around uncovering and reclaiming stories related to heritage sites – their past use and their future potential'[7]. Still, the organisers, all of whom were ethnic Albanians, did not act according to that idea in practice. During the short tour around Prizren, we went from the hammam to the Archaeological Museum and reached the medieval church of the Holy Virgin of Ljeviš (Figure 1), the endowment of King Milutin of Serbia in the fourteenth century. It was built in 1306/7 upon the remains of the thirteenth century cathedral, which had also been built on the foundations of an earlier basilica dating back to the ninth century. When the Ottomans converted the church into a mosque, probably in the eighteenth century, the existing frescoes (thirteenth to four-teenth century) were covered with mortar and whitewashed. The substantial readjust-ments that were made indicate that the meaning of the place was partially preserved, but 'upgraded' by changing the function and purpose of the building. When the Ottomans departed in 1912 the process was reversed, with the minaret being removed from the church in 1923 (Nenadović, 1963; Panić & Babić, 1975). Due to the aesthetic qualities ident-ified in this episcopal church from the fourteenth century, as well as the historical signifi-cance of the place, the Church of the Holy Virgin of Ljeviš in Prizren was declared a cultural monument in 1948 by the Republic Institute for the Protection and Research of Cultural Heritage of Serbia – Belgrade, and in 1990 due to the changed legislative was categorised

Figure 1. Church of Holy Virgin of Ljeviš in Prizren, fourteenth century (photo taken after 1953);. source: Institute for protection of monuments in Prizren

as a cultural monument of great importance (Pejić, 2007, p. 322). During the war in 1999 and later in 2004, the church was damaged.[8] Later on in 2006 the church was inscribed in the UNESCO World Heritage List and simultaneously to the List of World Heritage in Danger.

However, when the participants of the seminar in Prizren arrived at this church, their guide spoke about it with a different tone compared to his informed narratives about previously visited locations. He neglected basic historical facts in favour of new, unfounded allegations, and such change was surprising at least. However, the seminar participants, mainly coming from Western European countries did not react, even though they probably knew a somewhat different history of this place. The others, from the former Yugoslavia, conscious about the possibility of disrespect of the past, did not seem to know whether their reaction would reflect professional collegiality or personal conflict with the organisers of the seminar. On my initiative, the conversation about historical meaning of the Church of the Holy Virgin of Ljeviš was continued after the appointed guide concluded that there was nothing left to say.

The irony of this event is reflected in the fact that both the visitors and the guide in Prizren assumed expert roles in the field of cultural heritage and memory interpretation. The initial presentation at the seminar was focused on cultural tourism, but in actual life, in Prizren, we get a notion of heritage as disturbing, not a cohesive agent in a multicultural environment (as we agree as experts), so some of the historical facts should be ignored. This event could have likely been taken as an excursus justified by tiredness or the architect's lack of experience in guiding. Still, printed brochures that we got at the same occasion (see Basha, 2012), as well as other promotional material of the official Kosovo (see endnotes), make us think differently and observe the whole situation in a broader context. 'Heritage in everyday life', as Serbian museologist and art historian Popadić (2012) named his book, becomes a paradigm of social acceptance, understanding and the use of the past. The guide in Prizren and his (brief) exposure may reveal a real problem of instrumentalising heritage. Specifically, the presentation of the architect revealed that: (1) the best preserved heritage layers that indicate the Serbian history, are clearly suppressed and (2) the 'alienation of cultural heritage' is present, through emphasising the fictional and the real historical layers that indicate the Illyrian and Ottoman history as the principal foundation for the national and religious identity of Kosovo Albanians (Pavličić, 2015, pp. 120–121). If we take into account that the Virgin of Ljeviš was attacked in 1999 (Garić, 2002, p. 40) and again in 2004 by Albanian extremists, then we know that it could not have been perceived as 'their' own heritage, but as a Serbian Church. This trend of 'alienation of heritage' can be traced from the moment when this church, along with three other medieval monasteries, has been put on the UNESCO World Heritage in Danger List.

Therefore, if we consider the perception of these Serbian medieval monuments in Kosovo, the period since 1999 cannot be seen as integral. It has two phases, with the cutoff year flexible, within the period from 2006 to 2008, that is, between the inscription of the Serbian medieval monuments on the UNESCO's list and Kosovo's declaration of independence.

Heritage interpretation in the Kosovan tourist brochures

If we agree with the definition of heritage as 'contemporary uses of the past' or 'active processing' of the past, then the problem of understanding the idea of heritage is moved on to the problem of inheritance, as the process of preserving and transmitting the experience 'stored' in heritage (Bulatović, 2005). The 'figures of memory', such as narratives, texts, images, etc. have an ability to transfer the meanings of collective experience (Assman, 2001; Kuljić, 2006), so we will present some of the most representative ones relevant for our case study.

Official publications, in which Serbian medieval monuments in Kosovo are represented, are the best indicator of perception of this heritage in public memory. One of these is the tourist brochure 'Prizren, Kosova – The Visitor', published by the Municipality of Prizren, Department of Tourism and Economic Development in 2012. This publication is free of charge, and, as such, the most available to tourists. Since it comes from a public institution, it is believed to deliver reliable and accurate information. In the brochure, some basic facts about the state and society are followed by the history of the town and sightseeing recommendations. Although there are several medieval orthodox churches preserved in Prizren, which are also the oldest examples of architectural heritage from the period, only three of them are presented in the guide. Despite the fact that the Church of the Holy Virgin of Ljeviš was inscribed into the UNESCO World Heritage List several years ago, this information is completely left out in this publication. It has not got its rightful place among the monuments for being the oldest church in Prizren either – if we consider the *age-value* (Riegl, 1903). On the contrary, the description of this church comes only after information concerning the Sinan Pasha Mosque (seventeenth century), the Shadervan, the Prizren springs, the Whiteriver, the old houses (nineteenth century), the Catholic Church of the Helpful Lady (nineteenth century), the traditional clothing of Hasi, the (Orthodox) Church of St. George (nineteenth century), the tekke of tariqa Rufai, the bridges over Lumbardhi, the (Orthodox) Church of St. Savior (fourteenth century) and the Prizren Castle. It is interesting that this tourist brochure was written in very bad English and Serbian, and that it contains dubious information. For example, the Sinan Pasha Mosque is said to be from the eighteenth century, whereas it is from the first half of the seventeenth century, the church of St. Savior allegedly dates from the second half of the eighteenth century, whereas it dates from the fourteenth century (Bošnjak, 1959; Marković, Ristić, & Bačkalov, 2005). Also, the photograph of church of St. George is the wrong one. The most serious mistakes were made about the Church of the Virgin of Ljeviš and this text can be interpreted as the source for the aforementioned architect's speech, but also as a paradigmatic indicator of public opinion in Kosovo, and as such will be fully quoted:

> Church of 'Shen Premta' (Saint Friday) of VI–XIV century
>
> Many times before the arrival of the Slavs in Prizren, this church served as the pagoda to Dardania residents. This pagan temple was devoted to the goddess Illyria Prem-Friday, goddess of fertility. Later Christian invaders-Slavic-Orthodox, 'Saint Friday' turned into Orthodox church named in 'Sveti Petak' which in translation means the same 'Saint Friday'.
> In the second half of the XVIII century when Prizren was conquered by the Ottomans turns church into a mosque (1756) by adding the minaret and name 'Juma mosque' which in translation means – Friday. Later with changing of rulers, the minaret was removed from 'Juma mosque' and in its place put the bell and back again the name 'Sveti Petak'. (Basha, 2012, p. 44)

More detailed information about the church can be found on the official web site of the publisher – the municipality of Prizren,[9] but the 'Dardanian pagoda' is there changed into 'Byzantine'. Heritage appears to be of so little importance in public life that the authors could not agree even on basic facts. This is probably due to the fact that the experts from relevant scientific disciplines were not consulted. However, academic support for the thesis about the distant analogies between Dardanian history and the medieval church can be found in the book by archeologist Shukriu, 'Kisha e Shën Prendës', also published in 2012. Yet, her 'new scientific achievements' are quite problematic and have not been directly incorporated into the monument's interpretation. It is not only because they have not been widely accepted within the scientific community, but also because such distant analogies are not relevant for the visual qualities of the church, based on which it was categorised as a World Heritage Site.[10] The question of the name of the church, and the idea of hagiotoponym was marked even before, suggesting a completely different theory (Loma, 1989). But, it was never considered as significant in further research and evaluation of this monument.

However, the aesthetic, historic and age-value are just some of this monument's values, and they certainly do not satisfy, but should provoke our interest in it, as Alois Riegl noted in his seminal article entitled *The Modern Cult of the Monument: Its Character and Its Origin* [1903]. In the aforementioned presentations, printed and web tourist guides, the described monument is strictly seen as a religious object. On the tourist map of the same web site, the Church of the Holy Virgin of Ljeviš is marked as church without the UNESCO emblem.[11] There is no specially marked road to its location and, since it is in the densely built urban core, there is only a signpost with the drawing.

In 2009 the Tourism Department of the Ministry of Trade of Kosovo also published the map – 'Tourist map of the Republic of Kosovo' in which monuments were recognised only by their function. It is also noticeable that, when it comes to the orthodox churches and monasteries they are marked without an adjective.[12] The same organisation published a tourist prospect in the same year. It looks rather like a photo album, not as an official presentation of natural and cultural heritage. Gračanica is the only monastery mentioned in the prospect, but without a wider and precise explanation. The UNESCO emblem is missing.[13] The same Tourism Department of the Ministry of Trade with Industry of Kosovo (MTI) and the German Agency of Technical Cooperation developed the Tourism Development Strategy of Kosovo in 2006. This was examined to discover strategic consideration of the challenges of tourism development. The main challenges were political problems, limited expertise and professionalism, particularly due to political nepotism in staffing processes, which renders the problem of interpreting heritage much more complex.[14]

There are also several popular tourist web sites that refer to cultural heritage in Kosovo. One of them is a German widely known organisation 'In Your Pocket', which has, so far, published tourist guides of Prizren and Priština. *Prizren in Your Pocket* is produced in partnership with the aforementioned Swedish Foundation CHwB – Kosovo Office. This short publication contains more objective information, although in a very limited form dictated by the space available.[15] The same, but even shorter, is the one on the web site of Kosovo Tourism Center, the organisation that seems to be a non-governmental organisation.[16] On the first web site, the Church of the Holy Virgin of Ljeviš is still categorised as a church, although without any UNESCO promotion. It is mentioned only after the Prizren fortress. On the other web site it comes after the Albanian League of Prizren, the Prizren fortress and the Sinan Pasha Mosque. The situation is similar with presentations of the Patriarchate of Peć Monastery, Dečani and Gračanica, the three monasteries that are also on the UNESCO World Heritage in Danger List. The Patriarchate of Peć is the last on the list of recommended heritage in Peć on the web site of Kosovo Tourism Center. All monuments preceding it belong to traditional nineteenth century architecture.[17] The Gračanica Monastery is completely missing from the Prishtina promoting list and the Dečani Monastery is the only one properly presented, as the first on the list 'To See' in the Dečani Municipality. It is listed before kullas (traditional Albanian houses from the nineteenth century) and before the cemetery of Ramush Haradinaj (Kosovo Liberation Army fighter) family.[18]

However, these monasteries retained their monastic function as spiritual centres after the war in Kosovo. But, their position is not the same, neither geographically, nor in terms of social role. The Gračanica Monastery (Figure 2), King Milutin's last monumental endowment, is situated in the Serbian enclave, in the village of Gračanica, 5 km from Priština, the administrative centre of Kosovo and Metohija region. Today, Gračanica is a female Monastery, an active place of worship. The role of *tourist guide* here is in the hands of the nuns and orthodox community.

The Patriarchate of Peć Monastery (Figure 3) is an active female monastery located at the very entrance of the Rugova gorge near Peć. This complex of four churches is the spiritual seat and mausoleum of Serbian archbishops and patriarchs. The churches were built in the thirteenth and fourteenth centuries and possess a rich history of styles of medieval wall painting on their walls (Đurić, Ćirković, & Korać, 1990). However, it does not have any active role in the social life of citizens, only few of them being Serbs. In the official Tourist map published by the Municipality of Peć, the Direction for Economic Development – Tourism Sector, the Monastery is presented as religious heritage, of no great significance. The area is presented as 'wild mountainous region' with 'breathtaking landscapes'.[19] The Municipality of Dečani is also promoted as a tourist and recreation centre with fresh 'forests, multiple pastures, rich fauna, fresh mountain air'.[20] This corresponds to a new

Figure 2. The Gračanica Monastery, fourteenth century (photo taken in 2009).

Figure 3. The Patriarchate of Peć Monastery, thirteenth to fourteenth century (photo taken in 2007).

representation of Kosovo as 'a land of youth'.[21] The entire tourist offer is primarily oriented towards younger population as a target group. The international marketing campaign focuses on improving Kosovo's image – Kosovo the young Europeans.[22] The latest Regional Tourism Strategy for western Kosovo, which includes the Municipality of Peć[23] indicates that the Serbian Orthodox Church is not considered as a stakeholder, and thus part of history is completely omitted. For example, in 2012, Peć had the largest increase in the number of overnight stays in its hotels by domestic and foreign visitors. But, it has nothing to do with the two nearest UNESCO sites. These monuments are not even recognised as resources for cultural tourism. Archaeological discoveries of Illyrian and Roman sites in Siparunt, Dresnik and Rakoc, and architectural heritage of the 'kullas' are highlighted instead.

Prizren, Kosovo's 'cultural capital', is also promoted as a town 'with many summertime festivals and the prettiest city centre in the country. This old city with its young population is a great place to visit (...) or for a longer stay in the beautiful mountainous surroundings'.[24]

Perhaps this orientation towards youth and economic principle of tourism justifies the lack of a serious and precise discourse surrounding cultural heritage, especially the one referring to the Serbian presence in this territory or to the recent war and political chaos. This confirms that in wars, according to Bulatović and Milosavljević, heritage is destroyed when its bearers cease to exist and are replaced by new communities. In other words,

> when cultural heritage gets destroyed in wars, its values are preserved only by its guardians, never by those who succeed, because some of them, following the mode of possession, are equally destroying people and cultures, while the others, following the mode of ideology, are creating historical falsifications, invented traditions and new kinds of heritage. (Bulatović & Milosavljević, 1999, p. 238)

The case of the Dečani Monastery: (self)promotion

One of the biggest and most active monastic communities have been preserved in the Dečani Monastery (Figure 4), which is located 12 km from the city of Peć. The monastic catholicon is the largest medieval church in the Balkans containing the most extensive preserved fresco decoration.[25] Legitimacy given to this monument by the UNESCO World Heritage List in 2004 brought the confirmation of its universal values recommending its protection and asserting that its preservation is in the interest of the entire humanity. However, they are not perceived in that way, because the reasons that threatened this heritage have not changed. Croatian museologist Šola reminds us that heritage is *a priori* democratic in its nature, and therefore its appropriation and instrumentalisation is an intervention in public opinion (Šola, 2014, p. 78). Thanks to this idea the Dečani Monastery was brought in focus again. It was the first monastery printed in a series of three postmarks of Kosovo Post Direction in 2009.[26] It seems that the nomination of the Dečani Monastery for the UNESCO List resulted in Kosovo officials' heightened awareness about the endangered heritage, especially after the self-declaration of the independent state of Kosovo on 17 February 2008. Many European countries accepted its independence and encouraged the development towards European integration.[27] This certainly prompted the introduction of a new cultural policy in Kosovo, based on tolerance, multiculturalism and other European values.[28] It thus happened that the heritage from the UNESCO List gained new importance and came into focus again. However, even then, more comprehensive information about these monuments and their history has been omitted, and such behaviour was recognised in the Serbian public as heritage appropriation.[29] As already mentioned, the Dečani Monastery also has not been properly presented in official tourist publications in Kosovo, which speaks in favour of different politics of remembering: the one organised in the name of the 'return to national roots', and the

Figure 4. The Dečani Monastery, fourteenth Century (photo taken in 2012).

other facing towards 'European values', the respect of which is a prerequisite of successful integration. Nevertheless, the brotherhood of monks from the monastery has published a multilingual tourist guide (2007), which illustrates this monument's historical development. Although there are no official records about the number of visitors, the publication informs us of this location's growing popularity among different types of tourists. This monastery also has developed activities within the local community, primarily helping those in need, regardless of their nationality. These activities define a spiritual continuity of the place and designate monks as rightful heirs and guardians of this heritage.

It should be said that they respond to the principles of heritage protection as formulated in Yugoslavia, and also in the Republic of Serbia, after the Second World War – when the first Institute for Protection and Research of Cultural Heritage was established (Brguljan, 2006, pp. 47–71). One of the first actions was related to the Serbian medieval monuments in Kosovo and Metohija (Bataveljić, 1951, p. 207). After being subjected to scientific research and initial protection measures, the most important monuments (the ones that are on the UNESCO List today) got their *keepers and curators*. Their task was 'to convey, interpret and promote the values of the monuments'. Also, for the first time they started recording the number of tourists visiting these places. These monuments were seen as museums of Serbian medieval art.[30] At that time, travel guides, brochures and popular publications were written, edited or supervised by experts and art historians. There was heightened state of awareness of the need to improve the tourism offer through visits to monuments, achieved via intensive collaboration of tourism organisations and Institutes for the protection of monuments (Zdravković, 1982). It is interesting to note that the first tourist guide in Prizren, edited by Sreto Bošnjak, an art historian and the first curator of the Church of the Holy Virgin of Ljeviš, was entitled 'Prizren – town museum' and was published in 1959. The whole town was perceived as a museum, and this medieval church and monument was treated here as a museum object, which in a way anticipates the later development of museological theory. In 1962, the publication that promote museums in Yugoslavia, also listed Prizren as 'town museum' (Janković, 1962, p. 59). The Dečani and the Peć Monastery treasuries were listed as well. Emphasis and interpretation of monumental features increases their significance and introduces the concept of authenticity as one of the fundamental characteristics of the monument (Maroević, 2004, p. 141). Meanwhile, the monuments continued their lives in accordance with their primary purpose, therefore, mainly as orthodox monasteries and churches.

Conclusion: guide in accordance with heritage

The presented illustrations refer to the complexity of dissonant heritage in the newly established, partially recognised, state of Kosovo and its different interpretations in touristic promotion. National narratives are constructed in such ways that are silencing certain historical phenomena, which are not compatible with the given ideological frame, and selecting only the suitable ones. The destruction of the examined monuments, both physically (as in the case of the Church of Holy Virgin of Ljeviš) and semantically, emphasises their symbolic value. As rarely preserved material and spiritual achievements of the Serbian people, these monuments are powerful memories of war, of the people who are practically exiled from Kosovo, and of the complexity of historical changes. Their destruction, repression and instrumentalisation are the methods of modern iconoclasm

(Kolrud & Prusac, 2014). The 'intention', clearly recognised in this case, is what distinguishes modern iconoclasm from motivated vandalism as a barbaric act and a 'seemingly neutral' destruction (see Gamboni, 1997).

The politics of oblivion in Kosovo, as a cause of the act of iconoclasm, should be transformed into an active policy of memory, which should find its stakeholder in tourism. Meanwhile, it can be argued that tourism is used as a tool of modern iconoclasm. The potential that heritage interpretation through tourism affects the audience (not only the visitors of the site itself) calls for reconsideration of the role of tourism in cultural development. Also, it shapes our understanding of iconoclasm, on one hand, and dissonant heritage, as a consequence of the Kosovo case, on the other. In addition, it answers the key question addressed in this paper about the real danger that threatens this heritage.

So, what kind of protection and (tourist) promotion of heritage do we need is not only a question to be posed in war and postwar context, but also the question of understanding heritage as a discourse.

The integrity of the monument as a 'living being' that communicates requires organised protection, but it is still not on the agenda of the agents in charge of heritage protection (in a wider sense that includes cultural tourism, too). In the social verification of heritology, as the learning about the art of memory, it is taken for granted that the established system of protection (legal and technical) be upgraded with a predilection for social protection. Such reconsideration of the protection system would include the socialisation of heritage, not only as an ideological problem, but also as a codified system of individualisation of human values. It necessarily assumes that heritage is a social measure of values, and therefore that heritage is a public good. Every society articulates this awareness through defining public interest and common values, that is, by way of accepting a general consensus around issue of world heritage as an integral heritage: natural, cultural, economic, sustainable development (Bulatović, 2005, pp. 14–15).

However, in practice, technical protection is the latest range of protection. Tourism as a social approach is not a conscious part of it. There is a slight difference between interpretation and managing heritage in the academic sphere and (contemporary) tourism, even if they function and occur simultaneously. As Mc Kercher and Du Cros conclude (2012, p. 232) 'Sustainable cultural tourism cannot occur until and unless the promotion roles are integrated with conservation goals.'

Disclosure statement

No potential conflict of interest was reported by the author.

Notes

1. In this paper we will use both the terms 'Kosovo and Metohija' and 'Kosovo'. The first one is in line with the official policy of Serbia and refers to Kosovo as an Autonomous province and geographic area. The second term will be used to emphasise the position of the Serbian medieval monuments in the self-declared Independent state of Kosovo.
2. Example: Criteria for the selection of sites to be included on the UNESCO World Heritage list http://whc.unesco.org/en/criteria/
3. http://news.bbc.co.uk/2/hi/europe/371562.stm Retrieved 20 December 2014.

4. See more on: http://www.kosovo.net/default2.html Retrieved 1 January 2015.
5. http://whc.unesco.org/en/list/724 Retrieved 19 December 2014.
6. CHwB is an independent non-governmental organization dedicated to rescuing and preserving cultural heritage affected by conflict, neglect or human and natural disaster. The regional seminar in their organization entitled 'Past Stories and Future Memories' was held between October 28 and October 30, 2013 in Prizren.
7. http://chwb.org/albania/news/open-call-for-the-regional-heritage-seminar-in-prizren-kosovo/ Retrieved 19 December 2014.
8. See also: http://spomenicikulture.mi.sanu.ac.rs/spomenik.php?id=328
9. http://prizren360.com/en/what-to-visit/monuments/01-the-saint-friday-church-levishka# Retrieved 19 December 2014.
10. See the criteria on: http://whc.unesco.org/en/list/724/ Retrieved 20 November 2014.
11. http://prizren360.com/en/touristic-map Retrieved 21 December 2014.
12. http://www.mti-ks.org/en-us/Publications2 Retrieved 20 November 2014.
13. http://www.mti-ks.org/repository/docs/prospekti_eng.pdf Retrieved 20 November 2014.
14. The presentation of Shiperim Reka 'The importance of strategic tourism development in a post/conflict context' available on: http://www.regionalstudies.org/uploads/The_Importance_of_Strategic_Tourism.pdf
15. http://www.inyourpocket.com/kosovo/prizren/Sightseeing/Churches/Church-of-Our-Lady-of-Ljevis_62360v
16. http://kosovotourismcenter.com/prizeren.html Retrieved 20 November 2014.
17. http://kosovotourismcenter.com/peja.html Retrieved 20 November 2014.
18. http://kosovotourismcenter.com/decan.html Retrieved 20 November 2014.
19. Publication available on: http://www.pejatourism.org/en/pdf/informatori-turistik.pdf
20. http://kosovotourismcenter.com/decan.html Retrieved 20 November 2014.
21. Youngest population in Europe – almost 50% are under 20 years old.
22. See: https://www.youtube.com/watch?v=dQRGHAdQjR0
23. The document has been produced with the assistance European Union Office in Kosovo.
24. http://kosovotourismcenter.com/prizeren.html Retrieved 20 November 2014.
25. See: http://www.srpskoblago.org/Archives/Decani/index.html Retrieved 20 November 2014.
26. http://www.postakosoves.com/?page=3,31 Retrieved 20 November 2014.
27. See the list on: https://www.rks-gov.net/sq-AL/Pages/ShtetKaneNjohurKosoven.aspx Retrieved 22 November 2014.
28. Constitution of the Republic of Kosovo available on: http://www.assembly-kosova.org/common/docs/Constitution1%20of%20the%20Republic%20of%20Kosovo.pdf Retrieved 22 November 2014.
29. http://www.rts.rs/page/stories/sr/story/9/Politika/59021/De%C4%8Dani±na±po%C5%A1tanskim±markama±Kosova.html Retrieved 20 November 2014.
30. These information are known from the documentation of Archive of the Republic Institute for Protection of Monuments – Belgrade, Register 'Kosovo', Letter from the Director of Institute for Protection and Research of Cultural Heritage to the Council for Education (26 September 1951).

References

Assman, J. (2001). Verständigung über Geschichte und Repräsentation von Vergangenheit im alten Orient [Understanding of the history and representation of the past in the ancient Near East]. In H. Welzer (Ed.), *Das soziale Gedächtnis* (pp. 63–88). Hamburg: Hamburger Edition.
Basha, B. (2012). *Prizren, Kosova – The visitor*. Prizren: Municipality of Prizren, Department of Tourism and Economic Development.
Bataveljić, O. (1951). Kratak pregled rada Zavoda za zaštitu spomenika kulture NR Srbije [A brief overview of the Institute for Protection of Cultural Monuments of PR Serbia]. *Zbornik zaštite spomenika kulture, Knjiga 1, sveska 1*, 1950, 202–207.

Bevan, R. (2006). *The destruction of memory. Architecture at war.* London: Reaktion Books.

Bošnjak, S. (1959). *Prizren - grad muzej [Prizren – town museum].* Prizren: Narodni odbor opštine Prizren – Savet za kulturu i prosvetu.

Brguljan, V. (2006). *Spomeničko pravo [Monumental law].* Beograd: Republički zavod za zaštitu spomenika kulture.

Bulatović, D. (2005). Baštinstvo ili o nezaboravljanju [Inheritance or about unforgetting]. *Kruševački zbornik, 11,* 7–20.

Bulatović, D. (2009). Museology and/as Hermeneutics. In *Ivi Maroeviću baštinici u spomen, Spomenice, knjiga 2* (pp. 6–71). Zagreb: Zavod za informacijske studije Odsjeka za informacijskeznanosti Filozofskog fakulteta Sveučilišta u Zagrebu.

Bulatović, D., & Milosavljević, A. (1999). Baština i rat: cinizam nužnosti [Heritage and war: Cynicism of the necessity]. *Nova srpska politička misao,Časopis za političku teoriju i društvena istraživanja, posebno izdanje, 1,* 237–250.

Chastel, A. (1986). La notion de patrimoine. In *Les lieux de mémoire, II.2: La Nation* (pp. 405–450). Paris: Gallimard.

Đurić, V., Ćirković, S., & Korać, V. (1990). *Pećka patrijaršija [The Patriarchate of Pec Monastery].* Beograd: Jugoslovenska revija/Jedinstvo.

Faro Convention. (2005). *The framework convention on the value of cultural heritage for society.* Faro: Council of Europe. Retrieved from https://rm.coe.int/CoERMPublicCommonSearchServices/DisplayDCTMContent?documentId=0900001680083746.

Gamboni, D. (1997). *The destruction of art: Iconoclasm and vandalism since the French revolution.* New Haven, CT: Yale University Press.

Garić, Z. (2002). Urbano graditeljsko i spomeničko nasleđe Prizrena i okoline danas [Urban architectural and monumental heritage of Prizren and the environment today]. *Glasnik DKS, 26,* 40–41.

Janković, D. (Ed.). (1962). *Muzeji Jugoslavije [Museum of Yugoslavia].* Beograd: Savez muzejskih društava Jugoslavije.

Jokić, B. (Ed.). (2003). *Final report: Project urgent protection of natural and cultural heritage in Metohia: July 2001–June 2002.* Belgrade: Mnemosyne Center.

Jokić, B. (Ed.). (2004). *March pogrom in Kosovo and Metohia March 17–19, 2004 with a survey of destroyed and endangered Christian cultural heritage.* Belgrade: Ministry of Culture the Republic of Serbia/Museum in Priština (displaced).

Kolrud, K. & Prusac, M. (Eds.). (2014). *Iconoclasm from antiquity to modernity.* Farnham: Ashgate Publishing Ltd.

Kuljić, T. (2006). *Kultura sećanja. Teorijska objašnjenja upotrebe prošlosti [Memory Culture. Theoretical explanation of the use of the past].* Beograd: Čigoja.

Loma, A. (1989). O imenu Bogorodice Ljeviške [About the name of The Virgin of Ljevisa]. *Zbornik Filozofskog fakulteta, Serija A, knj, XVI,* 91–100.

Marković, R., Ristić, J., & Bačkalov, A. (Eds.). (2005). *Prizren carski grad [Prizren royal city].* Priština: NUB 'Ivo Andrić'.

Maroević, I. (1983). Museology as a part of information sciences. In *Methodology of museology and professional training.* Addenda 3. (Joint colloquium ICOM International Committee for Museology). London: ICOM.

Maroević, I. (1993). *Uvod u muzeologiju [Introduction to museology].* Zagreb: Zavod za informacijske studije. Filozofskog fakulteta u Zagrebu. It was translated and published on English as: Maroević, I. (1998). [Introduction to Museology – European approach]. München: Verlag Dr. Christian Müller-Straten.

Maroević, I. (2004). *Baštinom u svijet [Into the world with the cultural heritage].* Petrinja: Matica hrvatska.

Mc Kercher, B., & Du Cros, H. (2012). *Cultural tourism: The partnership between tourism and cultural heritage management* (2nd ed.). New York, NY: Routledge.

Mensch, van P. (1992). *Towards a methodology of museology* (Unpublished doctoral dissertation) University of Zagreb, Zagreb.

Monks of Decani. (Ed.) (2007). *Visoki Decani Monastery.* Decani: Visoki Decani Monastery.

Nenadović, S. (1963). *Bogorodica Ljeviška, njen postanak i njeno mesto u arhitekturi Milutinovog doba* [The Holy Virgin of Ljeviš, its origins and its place in the architecture of Milutin's time]. Beograd: Narodna knjiga.

Panić, D., & Babić, G. (1975). *Bogorodica Ljeviška* [The Holy Virgin of Ljevisa]. Beograd: Srpska književna zadruga.

Pavličić, J. (2015). Zaboravi i modeli zaštite: Crkva Bogorodice Ljeviške u Prizrenu [Oblivion and models of care and protection: Church of the Holy Virgin of Ljevisa in Prizren]. In S. Pajić & V. Kanački (Eds.), *Zbornik radova Umetničko nasleđe i rat & Muzika i mediji* (Vol. 3, pp. 111–124). Kragujevac: Filološko-umetnički fakultet.

Pejić, S. (Ed.). (2007). *Spomeničko nasleđe Srbije* [The monumental heritage of Serbia]. Beograd: Republički zavod za zaštitu spomenika kulture-Beograd.

Popadić, M. (2012). *Čiji je Mikelanđelov David? Baština u svakodnevnom životu* [Who owns Michelangelo's David? Heritage in everyday life]. Beograd: Centar za muzeologiju i heritologiju Filozofskog fakulteta u Beogradu.

Popadić, M. (2015). *Vreme prošlo u vremenu sadašnjem: Uvod u studije baštine* [Time past in time present: Introduction to heritage studies]. Beograd: Centar za muzeologiju i heritologiju Filozofskog fakulteta u Beogradu.

Riegl, A. (1903). Der moderne Denkmalkultus, seine Wesen und seine Entstehung. Vienna (English translation: Forster and Ghirardo. (Fall 1982) *'The modern cult of monuments: Its character and its origins'*, in *oppositions*, number 25, pp. 21–51).

Salazar, N. (2012). Community-based cultural tourism: Issues, threats and opportunities. *Journal of Sustainable Tourism, 20*(1), 9–22.

Shukriu, E. (2012). *Kisha e Shën Prendës-Prizren* [The church of Saint Prend – Prizren]. Prishtinë: Minstria e Arsimit, Shkencës dhe Teknologjisë.

Smith, L. (2006). *The uses of heritage*. London: Routledge.

Stransky, Z. (1970). Temelji opće muzeologije [Basics of general museology]. *Muzeologija, 8*, 37–74.

Šešić Dragićević, M. (2011). Cultural policies, identities and monument building in Southeastern Europe. In A. Milohnić & N. Švob-Đokić (Eds.), *Cultural identity politics in the (post-)transitional societies: Cultural transitions in Southeastern Europe* (pp. 31–46). Zagreb: Institute for International Relations.

Šešić Dragićević, M., & Rogač Mijatović, L. L. (2014). Balkan dissonant heritage narratives (and their attractiveness) for tourism. *American Journal of Tourism Management, 3*(1B), 10–19.

Šola, T. (1997). *Essays on museums and their theory: Towards the cybernetic museum*. Helsinki: Finnish Museums Association.

Šola, T. (2014). *Javno pamćenje. Čuvanje različitosti i mogući projekti* [Collective memory. Preserving differencies and possible projects]. Zagreb: Zavod za informacijske studije.

Tunbridge, J. E., & Ashworth, G. J. (1996). *Dissonant heritage, the management of the past as a resource in conflict*. New York, NY: J. Wiley.

UNESCO. (2003). *Cultural heritage in South-east Europe: Kosovo*. Venice: UNESCO. Retrieved from http://unesdoc.unesco.org/images/0013/001344/134426e.pdf

UNESCO. (2006). *Decision: Inscription on the list of the world heritage in danger (Medieval monuments in Kosovo)*. Retrieved from http://whc.unesco.org/en/decisions/1029

Vergo, P. (Ed.). (1989). *The new museology*. London: Reakiton Books.

Zdravković, I. (1982). Spomenici culture i turizam [Cultural monuments and tourism]. *Saopštenja, 14*, 263–267.

Archived material

Letter from the Director of Institute for Protection and Research of Cultural Heritage to the Council for Education (26 September 1951), Register 'Kosovo', Archive of the Republic Institute for Protection of Monuments – Belgrade.

Second World War monuments in Yugoslavia as witnesses of the past and the future

Vladana Putnik

Art History Department, Faculty of Philosophy, University in Belgrade, Belgrade, Serbia

ABSTRACT

Memorializing the victims of the Second World War was an important part of the cultural and political propaganda in the socialist Yugoslavia. The heroes and the victims of war were remembered through numerous memorials, finding their place in the collective memory of the Yugoslav people. During the socialist period, many school excursions were arranged, but for more than 20 years these memorial sites were dropped from tourist and educational programmes. Today, after the passage of time, it is possible to discuss a complicated collective past. In this paper, the phenomenon of the Second World War memorials, their significance in the socialist Yugoslavia, their decline during the 1990s and increasing popularity at the beginning of the twenty-first century are considered. By analysing the way contemporary society experiences socialist memorials, it can be further considered how they can be represented as an important part of cultural heritage. The main purpose of this research is to point out the significance of memorial parks in Yugoslav socialist society, as well as to define their status today and finally to suggest ideas for their interpretation and presentation today.

Introduction

By the end of the Second World War the Communist regime came to power in Yugoslavia, bringing the end to its Monarchy. After a short period of Soviet influence, the changing politics of Yugoslavia included several important events, such as the secession from the Soviet Union in 1948 (Calic, 2013), the forming of the Non-Aligned Movement in the second half of the 1950s and finally the politics of the 'Third Way' (2013). The 1960s and 1970s were considered as the 'Golden Age' of Yugoslavia. After President Tito's death in 1980, a power vacuum emerged (Klanjsek & Flere, 2013) which marked the beginning of the final disintegration of Yugoslavia in 1991.

Political turbulences influenced the perception of socialist heritage, especially monuments. In this paper I will consider the question of the Second World War memorials as socialist heritage and the possibilities of their interpretation and presentation through a multidisciplinary approach. The monuments *in situ* were visited and analysed using historiography and art theory as well as the secondary sources. An effort was also made to highlight the role of the Internet and mass media in the promotion of cultural heritage. The paper also presents five personal communications with citizens who were born and raised in socialist Yugoslavia on the subject of the Second World War memorials, which only represents the beginning of a wider research on the subject.

The construction of memory in the Second World War in Yugoslavia

Monuments to the victims of the mass death and destruction of war help a society cope with the agony of the war experience. The monument pays tribute and gives immortality to the ones that gave their lives to their homeland, and helps soften the pain of the survivors. Remembering the victims of the Second World War was also an important part of the cultural and political messaging of socialist Yugoslavia. The idea of constructing a specific Yugoslav identity greatly influenced the memorial sculpture and architecture of that period. The Communist regime built a very structured message from the war's history. The heroes' accomplishments were transformed into a powerful instrument for educating the society in creating socialism (Bergholz, 2007). The heroes and the victims of war were remembered through numerous memorials, finding their place in the collective memory of the Yugoslav people. The monuments, as an expression of the State's history and Revolution, constructed both the collective memory and the void (Cvetic, 2012). As politician Aleksandar Rankovic said, the monuments are a bond which rightfully interprets the past (Bergholz, 2007). During the first phase of commemoration, which included the period from 1945 until 1948, a new form of tradition had been invented for the 'consumers of the remembrance' (Bergholz, 2007); with the dominant artistic form that of socialist realism for the memorials. This visual representation was chosen due to the political visions of the leading Communist Party and its president Josip Broz Tito.

The government's politics became 'softer' and not so radically socialist in the 1950s. Cultural politics and art were recognized as important instruments for the strengthening of international relations (Cvetic, 2012). The goal was to create secular spaces, designed to offer a spiritual experience, without introducing a religious dimension (Chaubin, 2010). As a result of these events, a new aesthetic approach was developed by the name of 'socialist aestheticism'[1] (Denegri, 1993; Popadic, 2010). New design concepts for memorial sculpture also emerged. The focus turned away from the fallen partisan soldiers and to the civilians killed during the war, and reflecting the unity of the Communists fighting against fascism during the Second World War (Manojlovic-Pintar, 2014). The most eminent sculptors and architects in Yugoslavia were engaged in designing memorial parks, such as Dusan Dzamonja, Bogdan Bogdanovic and Miodrag Zivkovic. Their artistic language led to modernist universalism (Cvetic, 2012) and the creation of a new form of a 'place of memory'. The beginning of mass monumental memorial production in the concept of socialist aestheticism began with the anniversary of the Revolution in 1961. That year was marked by a massive production of monuments, including memorials in Prilep, Kragujevac, Banja Luka, etc. (Lajbensperger, 2013).

The period of 1960s and 1970s was mostly characterized by the homogeneity of the Yugoslavian cultural and historical tradition (Cvetic, 2012). During these two decades the production of extremely experimental memorials was often observed. The monuments were mostly marked by a metaphoric presentation and geometrical simplification of symbols (Baldani, 1977). The sculptures ceased to be anthropomorphic and became more 'free-formed' (Cvetic, 2012), with the concrete as the most used and popular material, primarily for its expressive structure, endurance and constructive quality (Miletic-Abramovic, 2007). The artists became more focused on the deconstruction of the form and its lack of description (Baldani, 1977). It was a 'bold' move towards abstraction, in accordance with the cultural politics of that period, which tended to encourage the avant-garde to show how artists in the socialist Yugoslavia were completely free to express their artistic creativity, in contrast to those 'behind the Iron curtain', where socialist realism was still dominant. As Juraj Baldani said, our most talented creators had caught up with the contemporary international artistic scene and became a part of it (1977).

Mass tombs of the fallen war victims were marked by monumental sculptural abstract compositions, pointing out in a subtle manner the horrors of war. They depicted the martyrdom of the partisans and the civil victims as sacrifices in the struggle against fascism and for the establishment of communism. The emotional potential of the memorial sites peaked with mass pilgrimage-like gatherings, student educative excursions and ephemeral events on important anniversaries, which were the essential elements of socialist ideology. The importance of the place where a battle was fought or a concentration camp held was especially emphasized, becoming the 'altar of the homeland', the holy grounds of the new socialist religion (Manojlovic-Pintar, 2008). Memorial parks sublimated the memory of the war by connecting the individual tragedy with a greater suffering of humanity through an abstract and associative artistic form, thereby creating an idealized image of the collective past. The vast open spaces in which the memorial sculptural compositions were placed also contributed to the sense of monumentality and the greatness of the war loses (Lajbensperger, 2013) (Figure 1). However, the monuments were not designed solely to glorify the past, but also the present (Cvetic, 2012). With that in mind, numerous ceremonies were held in the open areas of the memorial parks with several thousand visitors and radio and television coverage. At opening ceremonies

Figure 1. Miodrag Zivkovic, Memorial complex Kadinjaca, Serbia, 1979. (Courtesy of Vladana Putnik).

President Tito and other important politicians, such as Mosa Pijade, often held spirited speeches in front of hundreds of visitors (Lajbensperger, 2013). On the other hand, when there were no commemorations, many monuments and memorial sites also served as places of meeting and socializing for the younger generations (Bergholz, 2007).

In his work, one of the most eminent artists of this era, Bogdan Bogdanovic, probed and exploited the universal meanings of the symbols he used for various memorials dedicated to the victims of the Second World War. The primordial signs and symbols became a part of the unique Yugoslav cultural identity, but at the same time they represented a deflection from the ideological dogmatism (Manojlovic-Pintar, 2014). Many of the memorials he designed were places where commemorative ceremonies were held each year, such as Slobodiste in Krusevac, where the entire city participated in the programme as a way of strengthening patriotism (Manojlovic-Pintar, 2014).

These memorials became important symbols of the state, as places where young generations would be educated about the foundations of socialism (Karge, 2014). A memorial museum was also constructed as a part of each memorial complex. Although its programme often idealized the vision of the past, it undoubtedly played an important part of the educational process in Yugoslavia. Museums were places of the most direct contact between the past and the present (Manojlovic-Pintar, 2014). One of the most important centres of the collective Yugoslav memory was the memorial site Tjentiste, as the place where the battle of Sutjeska was held. The battle of Sutjeska represented one of the most important events of the Second World War on Yugoslav territory. The first monument was erected in 1949, then torn down to make room for a new one in 1958, and again enriched when the memorial complex finished in 1974. This symbol of the state, built in an inaccessible location, became one of the many obligatory places for the student excursions to visit (Manojlovic-Pintar, 2014). Apart from Tjentiste, numerous memorial parks became 'touristic attractions' of sorts (Moose, 1990), since they were the locations of increasing number of organized trips and tours.

A vast topography of places of remembrance illustrated the beginnings of the new socialist Yugoslavia. Each city had its own heroes, victims and memorials (Calic, 2013). Another important memorial site was Sumarice in Kragujevac. On the area of 352 ha, the memorial park was one of the most representative sites, with around 30 monuments in it (Manojlovic-Pintar, 2014). Its most known monument is dedicated to the pupils and professors who were shot by the German occupation army in 1941 (Figure 2). The monument is the work of the sculptor Miodrag Zivkovic (Putnik, 2014). The expressionist form of the monument became a symbol of the entire site Sumarice and it has been a place of annual ceremony for over 40 years (Lukovac, 2012). It can be concluded that through associative abstraction the tragedy of war became connected with the universal suffering of mankind. For that reason, Sumarice has not fallen into oblivion, unlike other similar complexes. Even today, the entire park is carefully maintained, as a way of paying respect to the victims.

The End of socialist Yugoslavia and the beginning of the devastation of monuments

The so-called 'charismatic leader' Tito had died in 1980 and there was no politician up to the task of inheriting a state that already had a large number of unsolved issues (Calic,

Figure 2. Miodrag Zivkovic, Monument to the shot professors and pupils of the Kragujevac Gymnasium, Serbia, 1963. (Courtesy of Vladana Putnik).

2013). An economic, political and social crisis quickly emerged during the 1980s, followed by inflation and a rapidly declining standard of living. These events caused an increase in unemployment, and heightening social unrest throughout the nation (Calic, 2013). On the other hand, the political situation slowly began to change. The weakening of self-management socialism led towards a turn to nationalism. The individual nationalisms, suppressed during the period of Tito's reign, returned and grew stronger during the late 1980s (Hayden, 1999). The nationalist political wings became dominant in most parts of the country. The Communist construct of the official Second World War remembrance slowly began to collapse (Bergholz, 2007) as well as social values such as equality, solidarity and self-sacrifice (Calic, 2013).

The last decade of socialist Yugoslavia was also marked by new interpretations of the events of the Second World War. The recently notorious Chetniks[2] suddenly became interpreted as equally important as partisans in the fighting against fascism. A discussion considering the number of victims that died during the war in concentration camps reopened (Calic, 2013). All these events brought to mind some of the painful experiences and memories of the war that have been repressed over the decades. The construction of monuments dedicated to the Second World War continued but declined until the beginning of the 1990s. During the 1980s the monuments were mostly erected for war events which were of less importance to the Communist party of Yugoslavia, such as the memorial complex at Sremski front, finished and opened in 1988 (Radulovic, 2011). Instead of Tito, other important political figures from that period had the honour to give a speech at the opening ceremony, such as Milka Planinc or Rados Smiljkovic (Lajbensperger, 2013). However, their authority could not replace Tito's and those openings had a very different aura, which in a certain way announced the unravelling that will end the existence of the socialist Yugoslavia.

The disintegration of Yugoslavia and the new political situation brought a change in what the monuments from the past socialist era meant for the new states and peoples. The civil war caused numerous negative reactions towards socialist heritage in general. The politicization of cultural heritage led towards revisionism and general denial of the socialist past in all former Yugoslav Republics. In such an atmosphere new romanticized identities of post-Yugoslav nations were formed. Glorifying the pre-Yugoslav past and negating the remembrance of a recent one, the political atmosphere led to incorrect treatment of the Second World War monuments. In that atmosphere of political and cultural autism new identities of nations emerged as a consequence of the desire to negate and purify memory from unwanted elements (Potkonjak & Pletenac, 2007). The political conflicts spread and reached all important spheres of society. The objects of memory suddenly became symbols of a problematic, conflicting and ideologically undesired past.

During the 1990s socialist memorials were often referred to as carriers of ideological design, which often outgrew their form and content. However, their symbolism was significantly more complex, since they have changed their role and meaning several times over the decades due to the turbulent political events. These changes caused numerous faulty interpretations of the socialist heritage, which led to a large number of memorials' destruction and decay throughout the last decade of the twentieth century. Monuments and memorial sites became places of conflict and the victims of violent behaviour through deliberate destructive acts (Etkind, 2004; Potkonjak & Pletenac, 2007). The aggression, religious and ethnic intolerance and frustration towards everything Yugoslavia represented up to that moment was applied through demolitions, displacements and political abuses of memorials. As the civil war became extremely brutal, so did the treatment towards the collective heritage. Buildings in war zones were deliberately torn down and historic centres were bombed, as well as important edifices, such as churches, mosques and libraries (Calic, 2013). Withdrawing symbols of socialist ideology and patriotism had a purpose to erase and reinvent the image of the past.

The problematic relationship towards the Second World War Monuments had been present even during the socialist period, and the cases of neglect and devastation can be followed back to the 1950s. These events showed that Yugoslavia was in fact ideologically divided even during the years of prosperity (Bergholz, 2007).

Memorials which were more fortunate have been left aside to just be forgotten, unlike others that suffered major damage and even total destruction, such as monuments in Korenica, Sanski Most, Kosute, Knin, Makljen, Kamenska and many others, mostly in the areas where the civil war was being fought. Memorial parks through the entire territory of former Yugoslavia, once places of field trips and ceremonies, became deserted, neglected and left to decay in the final years of the twentieth century.

The problem of interpretation

Before considering the possible paths of representing Yugoslavian Second World War monuments to the contemporary public, the question of adequate interpretation must be answered. In a discussion that happened during the 1980s on the issue of interpreting literature called 'Against theory', the question of 'proper' way of interpreting a work of art has been brought up as important (Burzynska & Markowski, 2009). American literary theorist Stanley Fish also asked a crucial question: 'Is there only one proper way of interpreting a work of art?' He argued that if there were only one way of interpreting art, no one would be interested in further engaging. Therefore, new forms of interpretation are always favourable, because the definite meaning of an artwork does not exist (Burzynska & Markowski, 2009). With that in mind, there can be an infinite number of possible experiences of one single work of art. This theory is not solely applicable to the literature to which it originally refers, but also other art forms.

In the case of monuments that are the subject of this research, it can be concluded, with little doubt, that they have been treated as objects of socialist ideology up until recently, but they can also be interpreted solely as works of art. A question arises whether these monuments can be looked upon as aesthetically composed sculptures deprived of any content or do they ultimately carry a message? Is this the sort of art which avoids posing any questions or accusations about the events of the Second World War? The political dimension is not the only one that can be perceived from the context in which the memorial sites were designed. Several cases of reinterpretation occurred in the first decade of the twenty-first century and they reopened the almost forgotten heritage.

One of the first foreign artists to offer a new vision of these monuments was a Belgian photographer Jan Kempenaers, affiliated to the University College Ghent Fine Arts. From 2006 until 2009 he travelled around former Yugoslavia trying to discover memorials from the socialist era. He was impressed by the abstract form of Yugoslavian monuments, their futurist design and artistic quality, since the knowledge of Western countries about art in Eastern Europe was mostly connected to socialist realism. Therefore, these memorials were experienced as something new, unseen and not typical for Eastern Europe. His project resulted in a series of exhibitions in Antwerp in 2007/8 and Amsterdam in 2010, and finally in a book called 'Spomenik', published in 2010. Kempenaers's work drew the attention of the world art scene, since it represented sculpture and architecture that were up until that point little known to the world (Figure 3).

In an interview for the online magazine 'Baltic Worlds', Kempenaers posed an important question:

> Can these monuments be seen as pure sculptures now, without the symbolism they represented when they were built? (http://balticworlds.com/symbolism-gone-for-good/)

Through this question it can be concluded that Jan Kempenaers's goal with these photographs was to show the public that Yugoslavian memorials can be seen from a different angle. It is especially interesting that a foreign artist, politically neutral, without any knowledge about the ideology or the past of these monuments, was the first to cast a new light on them and indirectly re-establish their meaning and importance.

In the preface for the book, Willem Jan Neutlings wrote:

> Looking at the photographs one must admit to a certain embarrassment. We see the powerful beauty of the monumental sculptures and we catch ourselves forgetting the victims in whose name they were built. This is in no way a reproach to the photographer, but rather attests to the strength of the images. After all, Kempenaers did not set out as a documentary photographer, but first and foremost as an artist seeking to create a new image. An image so powerful that it engulfs the viewer. He allows the viewer to enjoy the melancholy beauty of the Spomeniks, but in so doing, forces us to take a position on a social issue. The photographs raise the

Figure 3. Jan Kempenaers, Spomenik #1/Dusan Dzamonja, Monument to the Revolution in Podgaric, Croatia, 1967. (Courtesy of Breese Little Gallery).

> question of whether a former monument can ever function as pure sculpture, an autonomous work of art, detached from its original meaning. (Kempenaers, 2010)

The main problem of interpretation lays in this last sentence – Can monuments ever be pronounced as former? It is not a question that can be answered so easily, nevertheless it must be considered as important in the future of this part of cultural heritage.

The Internet also played an important role in the global popularity of Kempenaers's photographs. Websites, blogs and social networks reported about 'alien art', 'symbolism gone for good' and 'the end of history'. This phenomenon where a Western artist is being inspired by the 'other', foreign and exotic East is well known and its origins can be located in the romantic nineteenth century (Rauch, 2007). At the beginning of the twenty-first century numerous artists, mostly photographers, found their inspiration in the ex-Soviet and socialist countries and their art and architecture as something 'alien' to them and almost enigmatic. This quickly turned into a cliché where the post-Soviet world was depicted in decay. Another photographer, Frederic Chaubin, produced a similar monographic photo study 'Cosmic Communist Constructions Photographed' in 2010. By exploring and photographing architecture of the former Soviet Union, he revealed it to the Western world as something unknown to them. Chaubin referred to the architecture he photographed as 'exotic and unusual'. He also commented:

> Hence the strange purgatory in which these objects seem to float: so close in time and yet out of time. (Chaubin, 2010, p. 8)

This observation can easily be applied to the monuments dedicated to the victims of the Second World War in Yugoslavia.

Kampenaers's photographs became very popular and known around the world, but what even more important was that his art inspired further interpretations of Yugoslavian Second World War monuments. They very quickly became a sort of a muse to various new art forms. One of such projects is a film 'Sankofa', released in 2014 and directed by Kaleb Wentzel-Fisher. The idea of filming a science fiction film based on the lost memories of human kind was initiated when Kaleb Wentzel-Fisher read an article about Jan Kempenaers's photographs which inspired him.

Wentzel-Fisher defined his experience of monuments he chose to be in his film in an interview for a blog 'Artconnect Berlin':

> These bizarre and striking structures are hard to define, yet they were erected to serve as memorials to the victims and horror of the Second World War. Many of these sculptures look like abandoned alien ships, left to decay for the last two decades, if they weren't already dismantled by the government. The *Spomeniks* are a balance between architecture and something you may find in a museum. The intensely striking shapes and forms invoke a sense of wonder, but at the same time feel extremely haunting. (http://blog.artconnectberlin.com/2012/12/17/exploring-the-link-between-fictional-narrative-and-documentarysankofa/)

Presumably one of the most explicit examples of the director's use of the monuments as an inspiration in the film is the spaceship which is based on the memorial sculpture that was destroyed in 1995 in Knin, Croatia.

The worldwide recognition of the memorials' artistic values contributed to an affirmation in the domestic circles. Researchers began exploring them and writing articles on this topic, several exhibitions dedicated to this phenomenon were held during the beginning of the second decade of the twenty-first century. One such example is the regional project 'Unfinished Modernizations: Between Utopia and Pragmatism', which sought to explore architecture and urbanism of the territory of former Yugoslavia during socialism and their transformation to contemporary independent states. The project included both institutional and non-institutional sectors from Slovenia, Croatia, Serbia and Macedonia. This two-year interdisciplinary research resulted in an exposition held in several cities during 2012, including all capitals of the successor states. The result was not only the reconstruction an important segment of shared history, but also the strengthening cross-cultural respect and understanding through trans-national collaboration (Kulic & Mrduljas, 2011).

Another eminent example is the exhibition 'Monuments of revolution and people's liberation struggle of ex-Yugoslavia after the World War Two' by Branimir Prijak and Nedim Zlatar. It was held in 2012 in several cities on the former Yugoslav territory, including Belgrade, Sarajevo and Zenica. The authors' goal was to explore the past concept of collectiveness, 'brotherhood and unity' and today's tension created by fission of these territories. The result was a unique picture of relations between peoples and territories, their attitude towards this recent part of history, and the depiction of the monument's existence as a phenomenon in a certain territory (http://www.seecult.org/vest/spomenici-revolucije-i-nob).

One of the most interesting domestic art teams, which also can be a good example for this approach, is 'Yugodrom'. Though several innovative projects they explored the Yugoslav heritage. One of their projects, 'Greetings from YU', glorifies Yugoslavian Second World War monuments in the form of postcards (Figure 4). The idea was to emphasize their beauty by changing the original environment with an idyllic one, for example vast

Figure 4. Yugodrom, A postcard from the collection 'Greetings from YU'/Ivan Sabolic, Monument to the Resistance in Memorial park Bubanj, Nis, 1963. (Courtesy of Yugodrom).

horizons or crowded sea-sides, which symbolizes their persistence in a non-existing place as Yugoslavia is today. Monuments were positioned in beautiful beach landscapes with visitors and that photo-montage makes them look like hotels. Their touristic features have been emphasized, and the goal was to call for their preservation and indicate their historical value and interconnection. On the back of the postcards are the names of fictitious destinations while the description below gives the names of the real locations used in the collage. The artists retained the symbolic value of the monuments, simultaneously sending anti-nationalist messages to new generations (http://yugodrom.com/yupozdravi.html).

Approaching foreign and domestic tourists

As Willem Jan Neutelings observed, hardly anyone outside the former Yugoslavia was aware of the existence of such memorials. For him, it seems as if the memory has vanished and all that remains is pure sculpture in a desolate landscape (Kempenaers, 2010). It could be concluded based on the examples of several phenomena which recently occurred in the Western countries, foreigners that are not burdened by the Yugoslav past and ideology can see and experience its monuments in a completely different manner. Nevertheless, it is necessary to make a specific approach towards potential foreign tourists. Foreigners often do not see the ideological dimension of Yugoslavian memorials; since the sculptures are not figural or designed in the manner of socialist realism, but abstract. They give an impression of neutrality, but also a sense of unsolved mystery to the observer.

It might be difficult for Westerners bearing stereotype views towards Eastern Europe to comprehend the ideology of this art. Because they tend to see art first and ideology second, the narrative should be presented in such manner that the history of these sculptures as memorial places is not ignored. However, it might be appropriate to let foreign tourists feel the places of memory they visit and experience them emotionally as 'alien landmarks', 'objects of stunning beauty' or in any other way they wish. The important element is not to leave the visitor uninformed after he or she spiritually experiences the locations. It is essential to educate foreign tourists about the reasons why these monuments were designed, their history and purpose. Due to the online popularity of the monuments, there is already a tremendous touristic potential that has not yet being fully used. The key element towards raising the educational level about socialist heritage should be in regional projects and tours that would benefit the entire former Yugoslav territory.

With the domestic public, the situation is different. From the 1950s until the end of the 1980s entire generations of pupils and students were taken to organized student excursions to visit these particular places of memory (Cvetic, 2012, p. 318). But at the same time, even though many people visited memorial sites and participated in numerous ceremonials, they mostly held a distance towards the abstract monumental sculptural forms (Manojlovic-Pintar, 2014, p. 383). Hence a prejudice was formed towards the partisan and communist ideology. Younger generations whose parents fought in the Second World War were burdened by the importance of their sacrifice and could not entirely connect with the memorial sites and their significance for the Yugoslav society. In an interview with Z. P., a son of partisans, he underlines that in the period of socialism he thought about the monuments as a good and positive thing, however today he thinks that the large number of erected monuments led to loss of the true meaning of the memorial sites (personal communication with Z. P., 4 December 2014).

On the other hand, children whose parents were not members of the Communist Party of Yugoslavia referred to the memorial sites of that era as once important but outdated. They usually connect them with their youth, fond memories of student excursions and social fun. Although they learned about the Second World War, they never emotionally experienced the memorial sites as such. When asked about the impression the sculptures had on them, they replied that they think of them as monumental and impressive. They also thought that it is good that the monuments exist, because they reflect a period when everything was done in high quality and built to last, unlike today. Some of them are also conscious of the fact that the monuments were neglected due to the politics and not due to the lack of their quality and importance. They concluded that the beauty of those sculptures did not permit them to be forgotten (personal communication with M. M., B. P. and V. S., 4 December 2014).

After the disintegration of the socialist Yugoslavia, entire generations born and raised in what were now former Yugoslav Republics have not been educated about this chapter of their collective history. Places of memory became places of oblivion. An interesting fact is that interviewed citizens agree on the value of bringing back school excursions (personal communication with Z. P., M. M., B. P. and V. S., 4 December 2014). Some of them even suggested that parents should play a role in their children's education by encouraging family trips and visits to various places of memory (personal communication with Z. P. and V. S., 4 December 2014).

However, the post-socialist culture also brought a certain 'fashion of remembering' (Etkind, 2004). As historian Svetlana Boym referred, nostalgia often comes after revolutions or wars (Boym, 2001, p. 19), which is why the beginning of the twenty-first century brought several new forms of nostalgia, such as 'titostalgia' and 'yugonostalgia' (Mijic, 2011; Volcic, 2011). Since the transition brought uncertainty, many ex-Yugoslavs escaped into an idealized vision of the recent past. The longing for the 'good old times' of peace, unity and tolerance of the former emotional homeland brought an idolization of Tito and Yugoslavia. This phenomenon might be interpreted as a romantic yearning for a long-lost happiness and utopia (Calic, 2013). However, that concept could be considered as the key idea in the promotion of socialist monuments to domestic tourists, especially when a certain time distance has been developed.

Even though several decades have passed, the subject of socialist monuments is hot again today. For the ex-Yugoslavs socialist monuments are still marks of memories, either good or bad, and a very small percent of them think about these sculptures as work of art. Most of them, especially the generation born and raised in Yugoslavia does not believe that they have any aesthetic value. One way of approaching the domestic audience is to take the historic burden off and present the monuments as art, so they could see and experience them from another angle. This approach could help domestic tourists to be freed from prejudices they had towards the recent period of their history. Unfortunately, a number of citizens of the generation have no desire to go and visit these locations again (personal communication with B. B. 30 July 2015), although a certain number of them agree that school excursions should return as the old itinerary was a good educative programme (personal communication with Z. P., M. M. and B. P., 4 December 2014).

There is also another issue in regard to the complexity of the approach towards the domestic tourist. Although post-Yugoslav countries had the same socialist past, after the breaking up and the civil war, every country had a significantly different history, development and, more importantly, official interpretation of the recent common past. The fall of socialism led to identity disorientation (Stjepanovic-Zaharijevski & Gavrilovic, 2010). With that in mind, it is of great importance to define in which way domestic tourists should be approached and which is the right and most objective path towards the acceptance of the memorials dedicated to the victims of the Second World War as a part of their collective cultural heritage.

The concept of a cultural route could presumably be considered as the most adequate approach towards both foreign and domestic tourists. The European Cultural Route represents a road which bridges two or more countries or regions and it is focused on a topic which in historical, artistic or social aspect depicts Europe (Mangion & Tamen, 1998). The route must be based on a larger number of attractions. Cultural routes have been proved to be a good opportunity for touristic development. One of the benefits of this kind of regional projects would be the exchange and multidimensional dialogue between countries, as well as the engagement of local communities (Terzic, Bjeljac, & Jovanovic, 2014).

Conclusion

The almost iconic status these monuments had during the socialist period can still be found present in some parts of the new societies. The specific art language each author has in his own monuments is especially significant, although they all have the same approach towards the treatment of the public space and communication between the sculptural compositions and the natural environment, which makes them look as if they were at those locations since ancient times. They all managed to capture the zeitgeist and the artistic expression that transformed itself from the figural to the abstract (Baldani, 1977). The symbolism that is present in the work of Bogdan Bogdanovic, Dusan Dzamonja, Vojin Bakic or Miodrag Zivkovic is universal and timeless, therefore it is not necessary to interpret it solely through the socialist ideology (Putnik, 2014). Even though they should not be stripped off their initial purpose as memorials, their artistic status should be fully recognized as equally important.

There are approximately 12,000 monuments dedicated to the victims of the Second World War on the territory of former Yugoslavia, and they are all part of a valuable cultural heritage and also hold a tremendous touristic potential. Today, these monuments are still excluded from touristic and educational programmes. Post-Yugoslav Republics should begin treating memorial parks as their own heritage from the collective socialist past through an adequate conservation and revitalization programme. It is also necessary to become objective towards the collective memory considering the socialist past (Potkonjak & Pletenac, 2007). The concept of nostalgia can be considered as a key idea in the promotion of socialist monuments. Places of remembrance, which also represented targets of conflict, can be included in the process of forming a new image of cultural heritage in ex-Yugoslav Republics. Even though touristic development is important, Second World War Memorials should be returned to their primary function as places of memory. The individual and collective memory can be used for creating educational programmes and tours, not only for foreign tourists, but also for local citizens.

Today, when history can be looked upon as commodity, and therefore can be commercialized in order to gain profit with mass tourism (Manojlovic-Pintar, 2014), the potential programme for the touristic routes should be planned carefully and with high objectivity, distance and a scientific approach. It is concluded that there is no definite and one true interpretation, and with that fact in mind, the successor states should consider finding a wider audience for their collective Yugoslav heritage. That does not necessarily imply commercialization, but raising the level of the collective conscience and knowledge. As Katarina Schramm concluded, memorial landscape is never uniform or fixed and it is constantly reproduced by the ones engaged in memory revival (2011, p. 5).

Regional scientific research projects and exhibitions can also contribute to the rising level of consciousness about the significance our recent past has. A professional instead of a political approach and methodology can help improve this complex and delicate process of valorizing socialist cultural heritage. Through numerous scientific projects which would highlight the true value and timelessness of these historical monuments and sites, objective but attractive touristic programmes can be formed to educate and help in overcoming prejudice.

It is also crucial to include the local society into the programmes of revitalization. Places of remembrance should become the part of the process of forming a new image of cultural heritage in ex-Yugoslav Republics. The concept of cultural route has been recognized as the most adequate, since it involves touring several locations that are part of one phenomenon. Although most of these memorial sites were designed to provide additional contents (hotels, restaurants, etc.), they are not all commercial or approachable as individual tourist attractions (Terzic et al., 2014). Even though there should be different tours for various types of groups, these monuments should continue to be places of memory. With a professional approach the revitalization and touristic inclusion of Yugoslavian memorials dedicated to the victims of the Second World War is possible and necessary.

Perhaps the strongest message the memorials of the Second World War send is the heroic resistance of the man against evil through consolidation. The places of memory immortalized the victims and made an undoubted impact on the collective memory of the Yugoslav peoples. However, the memorials will stay silent and invisible unless they are visited and recognized as an important part of the collective memory and heritage. Future generations should be educated on these examples and taught not to forget and ignore their past. This approach is probably the only righteous path through which the monuments can continue 'living'. Bogdan Bogdanovic said for his monuments they had a unique message – 'life stronger than death' (Cvetic, 2012, p. 321).

Notes

1. The term 'socijalistički estetizam' was invented and defined by art historian Jesa Denegri in 1963.
2. Chetniks (Četnici) was a paramilitary organization who fought during the Second World War with the idea to preserve the Monarchy unlike partisans.

Disclosure statement

No potential conflict of interest was reported by the author(s).

References

Baldani, J. (1977). *Revolucionarno kiparstvo*. [Revolutionary sculpture] Zagreb: Spektar.
Bergholz, M. (2007). *Među rodoljubima, kupusom, svinjama i varvarima: spomenici i grobovi NOR-a 1947–1965. godine*. [Among patriots, cabbage, pigs and barbarians: Monuments and graves of NOR 1947–1965] *Godišnjak za društvenu istoriju [Annual of Social History]*, 1/3, 61–82. http://www.udi.org.rs
Boym, S. (2001). *Budućnost nostalgije*. [The future of nostalgia] Beograd: Geopoetika.
Burzynska, A., & Markowski, M. P. (2009). *Književne teorije XX veka*. [Theory of the XX century literature] Beograd: Službeni glasnik.
Calic, M. J. (2013). *Istorija Jugoslavije u 20. veku* [The history of Yugoslavia in the 20th century]. Beograd: Clio.
Chaubin, F. (2010). *Cosmic communist constructions photographed*. Köln: Taschen.
Cvetic, M. (2012). Monumentalna memorijalna politička skulptura. [Monumental and memorial political sculpture]. In M. Suvakovic (Ed.), *Istorija umetnosti u Srbiji XX vek: realizmi i modernizmi oko*

hladnog rata [History of art in Serbia XX century: Realisms and modernisms around the Cold War] (pp. 303–322). Beograd: Orion Art.

Denegri, J. (1993). *Pedesete: teme srpske umetnosti.* [The 1950s: Themes of Serbian art] Novi Sad: Svetovi.

Etkind. (2004). Hard and soft in cultural memory: Political mourning in Russia and Germany. *Grey Room, 16,* 36–59. doi:10.1162/1526381041887439. http://www.mitpressjournals.org/loi/grey

Hayden, R. M. (1999). Recounting the dead: The rediscovery and redefinition of wartime massacres in late and post-communist Yugoslavia. In R. Watson (Eds.), *Memory, history and opposition under state socialism* (pp. 167–185). Santa Fe, NM: School of American Research Press.

Karge, H. (2014). *Sećanje u kamenu – okamenjeno sećanje?* [Memory in stone – petrified memory]. Beograd: XX vek.

Kempenaers, J. (2010). *Spomenik.* [Monument] Amsterdam: Roma Publication.

Klanjsek, R., & Flere, S. (2013). Exit Yugoslavia: Longing for mononational states or entrepreneurial manipulation? In S. Flere (Eds.), *20 years later: Problems and prospects of countries of former Yugoslavia* (pp. 21–47). Maribor: Center for the Study of Post-Yugoslav Societies, Faculty of Arts, University of Maribor.

Kulic V., Mrduljas, M. (2011). Nedovršene modernizacije – između utopije i pragmatizma: Arhitektura i urbanizam u bivšoj Jugoslaviji i zemljama nasljednicama. [Unfinished modernizations – between utopia and pragmatism: Architecture and urbanism in the former Yugoslavia and the successor countries]. *Čovjek i prostor [Man and space],* 5–6, 4–9. http://www.covjekiprostor.net/hr/

Lajbensperger, N. (2013). Memorijali drugog svetskog rata u službi dnevno-političkih potreba socijalističke Jugoslavije. [The memorials of the Second World War in the service of daily-political needs of socialist Yugoslavia]. In A. Kadijevic & M. Popadic (Ed.), *Prostori pamćenja* [Spaces of memory] (Vol. 1, pp. 283–297). Beograd: Odeljenje za istoriju umetnosti Filozofskog fakulteta Univerziteta u Beogradu.

Lukovac, M. (2012). Uloga komemorativnih spomen-obeležja u konstrukciji kolektivnog pamćenja i društvenog identiteta. [The role of the memorial parks in the construction of the collective memory and national identity] *Nasleđe [Heritage],* 23, 201–210.

Mangion, T., & Tamen, I. (1998). *European cultural routes.* Strasbourg: Council Of Europe.

Manojlovic-Pintar, O. (2008). Uprostoravanje ideologije: spomenici Drugog svetskog rata i kreiranje kolektivnih parkova. [Spatialization of ideology: Memorials of the Second World War and the creating of collective parks]. In I. Graovac (Ed.), *Dijalog povjesničara/istoričara* [The dialog between historians] (Vol. 10/1, pp. 287–307). Zagreb: Friedrich Neumann Stiftung. Retrieved from http://www.cpi.hr/download/links/hr/11692.pdf

Manojlovic-Pintar, O. (2014). *Arheologija sećanja: Spomenici i identiteti u Srbiji 1918–1989.* [The Archeology of remembrance: Monuments and identities in Serbia 1918–1989] Beograd: Čigoja.

Mijic, E. (2011). Yustalgija: sećanje i materijalna kultura socijalizma kao okvir za konzumiranje sadašnjosti. [Yustalgie: Remembrance and material culture of socialism as a frame of reference for the consumption of the present] *Etnoantropološki problemi [Etnoantropological problems],* 6/3, 763–782. http://www.anthroserbia.org/Content/PDF/Articles/3ba794f2b98741c5bc6ac71f8a 613adc.pdf

Miletic-Abramovic, Lj. (2007). *Paralele i kontrasti: Sprska arhitektura 1980–2005.* [Parallels and contrasts: Serbian architecture 1980–2005]. Beograd: Muzej primenjene umetnosti.

Moose, G. L. (1990). *Fallen soldiers: Reshaping the memory of the world wars.* Oxford: Oxford University Press.

Popadic, M. (2010). Novi ulepšani svet: socijalistički estetizam i arhitektura. [New embellished world: Socialist estheticism and architecture]. *Zbornik Matice srpske za likovne umetnosti [Journal of Matica srpska for fine arts],* 38, 247–260.

Potkonjak, S., & Pletenac, T. (2007). Grad i ideologija: 'kultura zaborava' na primjeru grada Siska. [The city and ideology: 'Culture of oblivion' on the example of the city of Sisak]. *Studia ethnologica Croatica,* 19, 171–198.

Putnik, V. (2014). Memorijalna skulptura Miodraga Živkovića (period 1960–1980). [Memorial sculpture of Miodrag Zivkovic (period 1960–1980)]. In N. Zivkovic (Ed.), *Javni spomenici i spomen obeležja:*

kolektivno pamćenje i/lli zaborav [Public monuments and memorial sites: The collective memory and/or oblivion] (pp. 116–124). Beograd: Zavod za zaštitu spomenika kulture grada.

Radulovic, O. (2011). *Sećanja: Kako su se zavoleli krst i petokraka. Pakao u snežnoj ravnici.* [Memories: How the cross and five-pointed star fell in love. Hell in the snowy plain] *Ilustrovana politika* [Illustrated politics] Retrieved from http://www.ilustrovana.com/

Rauch, A. (2007). Neoclassicism and the romantic movement: Painting in Europe between two revolutions 1789–1848. In R. Toman (Eds.), *Classicism and romanticism: Architecture, sculpture, Art* (pp. 318–480). Cologne: Ullmann & Könemann.

Schramm, K. (2011). Introduction: Landscapes of violence: Memory and sacred space. *History and Memory*, *23/1*, 5–22. doi:10.2979/histmemo.23.1.5. http://www.jstor.org/stable/10.2979/histmemo.23.1.5

Stjepanovic-Zaharijevski, D., & Gavrilovic, D. (2010). Identiteti i porodične vrednosne orijentacije na Balkanu. [Identities and family value orientations in the Balkans]. *Sociologija*, *52*, 23–40. doi:10.2298/SOC1001023S. www.komunikacija.org.rs/komunikacija/casopisi/sociologija/index_html?stdlang = ser_lat

Terzic, A., Bjeljac, Z., & Jovanovic, R. (2014). Zaštita, revitalizacija i upotreba nasleđa kroz sistem formiranja kulturnih ruta. [Protection, revitalization and usage of heritage by forming a system of cultural routes]. *Kultura*, *14*, 319–335. doi:10.5937/kultura1443319t. http://www.zaprokul.org.rs/CasopisKultura/

Volcic, Z. (2011). Post-socialist recollections: Identity and memory in former Yugoslavia. In H. Anheier & Y. R. Isar (Eds.), *Heritage, memory & identity* (pp. 187–199). London: SAGE.

Tourism and the 'martyred city': memorializing war in the former Yugoslavia

Patrick Naef

Department of Geography and Environment, University of Geneva, Geneva, Switzerland

ABSTRACT

The present contribution aims to propose a definition of what is often referred to as a 'martyred city', a notion widely used in the media and the public sphere, but still largely understudied in academia. By looking at two cities in the former Yugoslavia – Sarajevo and Vukovar – this article presents the way in which a place can be associated with the notion of martyrdom through memorial sites and practices, such as war museums and tourism. The 'martyred city' is a way to memorialize past traumatic events, but also a means to achieve diverse agendas and objectives. It is finally stated that the distinction between 'victims' and 'martyrs' is often blurred, and a shift from the former to the latter can be observed.

Representing martyrdom

After or during violent events such as wars, sieges or bombings, certain places around the world have been designated as 'martyred cities'. Sites marked by a traumatic past – Hiroshima, Auschwitz, Guernica, Verdun, or more recently Fallujah in Iraq and Homs in Syria – have been labelled as such in the media or in the public sphere.[1] Martyrdom can also be expressed and experienced through material sites like memorials and museums, as well as through cultural practices such as commemorative ceremonies, artistic performances or tourism.

The notion of 'martyred city' generally implies the dissemination of a message, often linked to the mantra 'never again' (like in Auschwitz), but can also be related to more concrete narratives, for instance calling into question the whole nuclear technology altogether (like in Hiroshima). Furthermore, a critical issue is often linked to the designation of a group (national, ethnic, religious) as martyr, most of the time in opposition to one or more groups considered as 'enemy' or 'perpetrator'.

However, if the 'martyred city' designation has been largely mobilized in general media, a more attentive analysis of this notion in academia has yet to be undertaken. This contribution aims to fill this gap by proposing a conceptual definition, from an anthropological and geographical perspective, and by looking at the way in which some places in former Yugoslavia have been associated with the notion of martyrdom after the 1990s wars.

Furthermore, special attention will be given to the resurging tourism sector in the region, emphasizing the roles of narratives and representations of martyrdom in national and local tourism promotion. Finally, this contribution aims to demonstrate that the distinction between victimhood and martyrdom is often blurred, allowing certain 'memorial entrepreneurs' to present victims as martyrs.

When we look closely at the designation of 'martyred city' in the media, we can note that it usually refers to places at war as opposed to post-war settings. In examining the memorialization process in two sites in ex-Yugoslavia – Sarajevo in Bosnia-Herzegovina and Vukovar in Croatia – the main objective is to describe the ways in which those places are still represented as 'martyred cities' even after the armed conflict is over. In another geographical context, the case of Oradour-sur-Glane in France is a paradigmatic example, as it was officially named a 'martyred village' after the Second World War and the infamous massacre that took place there.[2] However, this designation refers to the preserved and uninhabited ruins, not to the new settlements built after the war next to the destroyed village. This is a fundamental difference when analyzing this dynamic in the context of living environments, like Sarajevo or Vukovar.

Those two places, and even more the symbols that they constitute now, are largely part of the founding myths present in Bosnian and Croatian independence narratives, in a similar vein to the way in which a village like Oradour was mobilized in discourses on post-war France. But unlike Oradour, these places are still inhabited, confirming that a 'lieu de mémoire' (Nora, 1997) can also constitute a living environment. In the context of Bosnia and Croatia, different national groups are sharing the same territory, causing numerous social conflicts. Therefore, any analysis of these martyred cities needs to take into account the division context and the nationalist discourses present in the former Yugoslavia.

Martyrdom and tourism

Tourism is far from being apolitical. Many scholars have already underlined the way in which tourism narratives can be vectors for ideology (Alneng, 2002; Moynagh, 2008; Naef, 2014; Pretes, 2003; Rodriguez, 2014). Rodriguez emphasizes the way General Franco exploited tourism during the Spanish war to represent Republican guilt in opposition to Francoist victimhood. Referring to the town of Guernica, she highlights the way this symbol of destruction was used in Francoist patriotic discourse and mobilized in opposition to Republican denunciations:

> Franco and Bolín[3] diffused the idea that Republicans burned the city in a ground attack and made people believe in the guilt of the opponent. […]. To underline the providential nature of Franco's war, those visits were a means to develop religious and patriotic rituals […].[4] (Rodriguez, 2014, p. 2013)

Guernica, now an important symbol of war, was represented as a 'martyred city' in order to serve Franco propaganda directly after its destruction, with tourism serving as the means to do so.

Yet, if several authors have included the notion of 'martyred city' in their work, its close examination is still very limited and totally absent in academic tourism studies. In the broad field of memory studies, Oliver-Smith (1986) used it as a title for his book, yet without analyzing it. He looked at the 'rebirth' of the town of Yungay in central Peru, which was destroyed by a huge avalanche that killed thousands of inhabitants in the 1970s. However, the cause of the destruction was natural and the issues related to its memorialization were undoubtedly quite distinct from those following human-caused tragedies such as wars. In this context, Bennett-Farmer (2000) conducted a historical study of the aftermath of the massacre in Oradour, looking at commemoration and legal matters and offering some very important insights on the representation of victimhood in French narratives.

In the former Yugoslavia, the 'martyred city' designation was widely used during the wars of the 1990s, especially when Sarajevo and Vukovar were besieged. A decade later, Bosnia and Eastern Croatia became paradigmatic case studies in general post-war research, and this analogy was occasionally introduced. Sepic, Biondic, and Delic (2005) analyzed the reconstruction of Slavonia and described the town of Vukovar after the siege as 'a martyr-town, a phantom town, a symbol of all the war destruction in Croatia'.

Yet the most important work related to the notion of 'martyred city' is without doubt Baillie's research on Vukovar's religious heritage. In her description of the city after the war in Croatia, Baillie (2013, p. 120) challenges the distinction between 'wartime' and 'peacetime', asserting that the place lingers in the limbo of conflict time illustrated by its persisting divisions and tensions: 'Vukovar's post-"reintegration" memorials have sought to remake and re-narrate the political landscape of the city – to express the Croat discourse of "victory through victimhood" in order to negate the RSK[5] discourse of liberation.' She adds that Vukovar became a 'martyred city' for the whole Croatian nation: 'a cityscape sacrificed for the creation of the nation; an urban landscape "hallowed by the blood" of victims and defenders' (Baillie, 2013, p. 300).

Defining the 'martyred city'

The conceptual framework that I propose here aims to highlight three distinct but interrelated dynamics. The first involves a memoryscape focused on a specific collective trauma, such as a massacre, war or siege. In other words, museums, memorials and other symbolic representations are largely oriented towards a historical and violent event. Secondly, some places tend to be designated as symbols of these events and mobilized in national and popular narratives.

Auschwitz is generally presented as a paradigmatic example when looking at the symbolization of a collective trauma. Assman (2010) for instance demonstrates how the material site of Auschwitz, after becoming a global symbol of the Holocaust, becomes disconnected from its historical context. Quoting Marchart et al., she notes that this symbolization process can lead to the site's instrumentalization: 'As the process of universalization of the Holocaust has emptied the symbol of its particular historical meaning, it can be used to legitimate everything including its opposite' (in: Assman, 2010, p. 114). For Nora, war, totalitarianism, genocides and crimes against humanity became dominant images in what he describes as the 'age of memory', adding that Auschwitz memorialization leads to what is now considered a 'duty of memory'.[6] As one can see, the material space of a traumatic and violent event can evolve into a symbolical space, a process that implies their disconnection: the symbolic Auschwitz spreading far beyond the material one.

Finally, the third dimension of the 'martyred city' is attached to the notion of martyrdom in opposition, for instance, to the one of resistance. Doss (2010) states that victims are now commemorated more than heroes. Yet the main issue of how to define heroes, victims or martyrs remains. Bennett-Farmer notes that the notion of martyrdom often implies a lack of resistance capacity in the face of the enemy. In her view, that is how Oradour victims were presented, and by extension, the whole image of France propagated in accordance with the memorialization of this massacre: '[…] the term martyr reflected the overwhelming belief that France had been powerless in the face of the Nazis' (Bennett-Farmer, 2000, p. 88).

Victim or martyr?

The link between martyrdom and lack of resistance capacity needs to be questioned. It seems that victimhood and martyrdom, often used to convey the same meaning, can nevertheless imply distinct representations. The notion of martyrdom denotes a form of will and an involvement for a cause, introducing the idea of individuals scarifying themselves for this cause (e.g. independence). In opposition, victimhood implies a lack of the capacity to resist and, above all, an absence of choice. Furthermore, Bennett-Farmer (2000, p. 88) also demonstrates that, in the case of Oradour, martyrdom was linked with a form of power associated with 'moral superiority': 'Martyrdom, which suggests physical weakness but moral superiority, implies a sacred cause – in this case, the cause of the nation.'

Riaño-Alcalá (2006, p. 123) defines the notion of martyrdom as 'an act of dying understood as a sacrifice made for the freedom and liberty of others'. She quotes Zulaika (1995) who presents the martyr as an 'activist' ready to give his own life as a genuine expression of commitment to his people. The myth of the martyr would be 'a historical model of masculine heroism that locates its roots in a mythology of sacrifice, and is supported by actions'. In opposition, civilian victims, like those in Oradour, were killed regardless of their actions or commitment and thus cannot be included in this definition of martyrdom, as it implies a form of agency.

It is stated here that dynamics involved in the 'martyred city' can lead to a shift from the status of victimhood to one of martyrdom in order to fulfil specific objectives, like presenting the moral superiority of a national group and stigmatizing another group (martyrs in opposition to perpetrators). In other words, could 'victims', after their disappearances, become 'martyrs' against their will, or at least without consideration of their will? This is of course crucial when looking at civilian deaths in opposition to military forces losses, the latter being characterized by a form of agency implying a commitment to a cause. It goes without saying though, that the soldier's agency – his or her voluntary involvement – may be strongly nuanced, as many soldiers are enrolled without their consent or have been warring for reasons largely disconnected from the cause they are supposedly fighting for.

In any case, Oradour commemorations attest to such a shift, insofar as its inhabitants, mostly women and children, certainly did not choose to be victims or raised as martyrs of the French nation. Their status as victims has thus been hijacked and transformed into one of martyrs in order to consolidate the national identity of a country in reconstruction. This is partly confirmed by Bennett-Farmer (2000, p. 10), who demonstrates how this notion of martyrdom has been integrated into the French memorialscape after the war through commemorative ceremonies and memorials:

> The story of innocent villages massacred by the Nazis implicitly gave the message that, regardless of their political choices or wartime loyalties, every French person was at risk and

potentially a martyr. The Resistance has received the most attention in official remembrances of the Second World War, but Oradour provides an alternative, symbolizing the victimization of unengaged French people rather that those who opposed the oppressor.

Turning victims into martyrs can thus be considered as a way of nationalizing – and dehumanizing – the dead by transforming individuals into patriotic symbols.

Finally, this memorial dynamic can also be related to the religious dimension of martyrdom, particularly with regard to the Catholic doctrine. Baillie (2013, p. 125) looks at the dissemination of Catholic symbols in Vukovar after Croatian forces recovered their lost territories in 1995, pointing to the sacred dimension it added to the city:

> In Vukovar, the 'sacred nature' of these sites is reinforced through the use of religious symbols (e.g. crosses) and the contribution made by the priest (e.g. special masses, processions, other rites). Collectively, Vukovar's Croat dead are depicted as innocent victims/heroes.

For her, by making their subjects sacrosanct, these memorials buffer them from critics, rending Croats beyond reproach.

Before going into further development, it is important to bear in mind that the constitution of the 'martyred city' depicted here is a process, to which cities can relate at various levels. The 'martyred city' is an abstraction – a conceptual frame – insofar as a martyred city does not exist *per se*. It is, of course, impossible to imagine a city where the totality of the memorialscape is determined by just one historical event, even the most traumatic. Therefore, the objective here is less to define whether or not a place is a 'martyred city', but more to show the degree to which it integrates this conceptual frame. Certain places like Auschwitz, Hiroshima or Oradour can already be introduced as paradigmatic illustrations of this process.

Touring the 'martyred city'

Oradour can also illustrate the touristification of a place associated with the notion of martyrdom. If at first it incorporated commemorative and testimonial dimensions of martyrdom, in that the ruins of the village were voluntary conserved, tourists started to flow once the war was over. According to a collaborator of the visiting centre, the number of visitors has remained stable for the past 50 years, ranging between 90,000 and 110,000 every year (personal communication, 05.10.2011). However, aside from the fact that the ruined village was no longer inhabited once it was turned into a site of memory, its touristic dimension also developed after its official designation as a 'martyred village'. Yet in the context of the former Yugoslavia, it is particularly the touristification of places, but above all, of their war cultural heritage, that contributed to their constitution as 'martyred cities'.

Looking at the place of fear in urban centres like Berlin, Neil (2001, p. 826) asks how a city 'twinned with hell', labelled as the 'capital of remorse', can be touristically promoted:

> In short Berlin's place marketing is plagued by a tension between distancing the city from the fears conjured up by the city's Nazi past but still finding an acceptable way to confront and keep alive the memory of this awful reality.

The case of Berlin demonstrates the tensions involved when tourism promotion and traumatic heritage are at stake. Concretely, it is exemplified by Breindersdorfer (2011) and Sion (2008) who highlight some site-use conflicts at the *Memorial to the Murdered Jews of Europe*, where sorrow clashes with touristic or daily practices like sunbathing, picnicking or biking, more associated with leisure than memory.

The purpose here is not to engage in a moral debate on the practices and uses suitable for such places. The examples of Oradour and the Berlin Memorial aim to point to the issues involved in the memorialization of extreme traumas, transforming places into icons of evil or suffering, and the more trivial practices attached to them, like tourism, or simply daily life routine. When a 'martyred city' is also a living environment, the site-use conflicts may become much more problematic. Bennett-Farmer (2000) also demonstrates that tensions can even increase when commemorative practices are initiated by external agents; in the case of Oradour, the French State's actions led to numerous oppositions from the local population.

An intense promotion of war heritage can be observed in different regions, such as in parts of France, Vietnam, Cambodia or Poland, where some places can be integrated in the 'martyred city' framework. Margolin (2007) notes about the Cambodian capital, Phnom Penh, that in a city 'which counts only a few landmarks, "genocide tourism" became a must'. Building on this idea, do traumascapes that are initially weakly promoted on the tourism scene tend to rely upon this war heritage, and thereby contribute to the 'martyred city'? That is what is implied in Topol's (2012, p. 124) cynical and burlesque novel – *The Devil's Workshop* – when the integration of Belarusian traumatic history in the tourism sector is advocated by one of the characters in order to transform the country into the 'Jurassic Park of horror and the eco-museum of totalitarism':

> You know how many tourists Belarus gets every year?
> 3'500 whispers Marouchka since I have no idea at all.
> 'It is time for change' says Arthur. 'You know which country had the most people killed? Here! You know in which country communists killed the most people? Here! Do you know where people keep on disappearing? Here! So isn't it a unique country? Exactly! A globalised world means role repartition for God's sake! Thailand for sex, Italy for the See and the paintings, Netherlands for the cheese and the clogs, and Belarus for horror trips.'[7]

Sarajevo and Vukovar memorialscapes and emerging touristscapes are largely based on their traumatic history, allowing them to incorporate the 'martyred city' framework. As it is postulated, sites and objects of memory attached to armed conflict, highly promoted within the tourism sector, contribute to the constitution of 'martyred cities' in the former Yugoslavia.

Furthermore, in places where different national groups that opposed each other during the war then share a territory afterwards, the 'martyred city' can contribute to the perpetuation of conflict by crystallizing national identities on, thereby harming any reconciliation dynamic. Conversely, the context of such post-war divisions also contributes to the 'martyred city' condition through the construction and reinforcement of war categories, often limited to the ones of martyrs, victims and perpetrators; this dynamic can lead to conflictual representations between a group belonging to the 'martyred city' and other groups considered as perpetrators or enemies.

As Viejo-Rose (2011, p. 47) underlines, memory conflicts attached to war categories can perpetuate violence cycles a long time after the official end of a war: 'Memory battles and competitions for victimhood are destructive; reconciliatory memorials would have to, in both intent and impact, release societies from cycles of violence fuelled by the legacies of the past conflicts.'

Martyred cities in former Yugoslavia

Sarajevo and Vukovar both lived through terrible sieges during the wars of the 1990s. The capital of Bosnia-Herzegovina was besieged from 1992 to 1996, and it is estimated that approximately 10,000 people were killed during this time. Vukovar was under siege for three months, from August to November 1991, and was defended by a few thousand *bra-niteljis*.[8] In both cases, the besiegers were composed predominantly of Serbian paramilitaries and militias, and supported by the Yugoslavian national army,[9] which also progressively became dominated by Serbs.[10]

Two decades after the end of the wars in Croatia and Bosnia, the two cities are now living in a context of division. This is institutionalized by a demarcation line in Sarajevo,[11] while in Vukovar, it is lived through a high level of political and social tensions between Croatian citizens and the large Serbian minority who stayed in the city once it was reintegrated into Croatian territories in 1998. However, since 2000, the two places are also experiencing the return of tourists to varying degrees. Vukovar was primarily visited by Croatian tourists, many of them coming to pay tribute to this important symbol of Croatian independence, progressively followed by more international visitors. Sarajevo, already a relatively important touristic city destination before the war, saw the reappearance of a significant number of international and local tourists in 2005.

Places as war symbols

During and after the armed conflicts, Sarajevo and Vukovar became important symbols. First, at a national level, they represented the struggle for independence of Bosnia and Croatia. Second, on a global level, they also rapidly became iconic images of suffering and resistance, in a similar vein to how Auschwitz is now a paradigmatic illustration of collective trauma.

Vukovar and its links to independence and war are symbolized in popular music (Baker, 2009), history textbooks (Höpken, 2007; Najbar-Agičić and Agičić, 2007), commemorative ceremonies (Kardov, 2007), religious heritage (Baillie, 2011), stamps, street names and banknotes (Naef, 2013), and of course in the military sphere (Naef, 2014). Furthermore, large signs representing former *braniteljis* are disseminated around the region of Slavonia, where the town is situated, and many inscriptions and graffiti remind the passers-by of the iconic status of the place (Naef, 2012).

In 2011, the president of the parliament even suggested the creation of a central site dedicated to the siege, that would be 'mandatory' for all schoolchildren across the country to visit: 'A place where they could learn about the war in Vukovar and the role [of] Vukovar itself, which was crucial for the establishment of the Republic of Croatia' (personal communication, 18.08.2011). Kardov also notes that between 1993 and 1994, some Croatian citizens suggested keeping Vukovar destroyed and fenced in as a monument, similar to what has been done for Oradour. He adds that from this moment 'it was perfectly clear that Vukovar occupied a significant place in national memory' (Kardov, 2007, p. 66).

In neighbouring Bosnia, Sarajevo received a wide echo in the international media during the siege, along with a relatively important resonance in popular culture (Naef, 2013). However, Causević (2008, p. 282) supports the idea that Sarajevo lost its place in the media once the war was over, 'except when there was a story directly related to the conflict'. This is partly confirmed in the field by one of the founders of *Green Visions*, a tour operator in Sarajevo, who underlines that Sarajevo is always put in relation to war, in Bosnia or elsewhere:

> Bosnia keeps popping up in the media. For instance, the *Daily Telegraph* titled an article on 'wild frontiers': 'British are going to war zone', quoting countries like Sudan and Bosnia in the first line. But when you read the article there was nothing on Bosnia. And the *Guardian* made a parallel about what is going on now in Libya[12] [...] and the Sarajevo siege. That had nothing to do, but it is so easy for people to use Bosnia as a headline. (personal communication, 24.08.2011)

Moreover, the Sarajevo Symbol recently came back on the front stage, when in 2014 the centennial of the First World War outset was commemorated in Bosnia. In this context, conflictual and opposed commemorative ceremonies organized in both entities – the Federation of Bosnia-Herzegovina run by Bosniaks and Croats and the *Republika Srpska* run by Serbs – demonstrated that the reconciliation process in the country was far from being achieved.

Setting the martyrscape

In Croatia, the city of Vukovar and the region of Slavonia are considered to have the largest number of monuments related to the last war (Baillie, 2013). The *Ovčara* Memorial Centre, the Museum *Vukovar Hospital 1991*, the Cemetery for Croat defenders and the water tower[13] constitute without doubt the most prominent and promoted sites. Furthermore, Vukovar, a city with less than 30,000 inhabitants, counts six cemeteries, all differentiated by religious or national affiliations.

Baillie (2011) conducted an in-depth analysis of cultural heritage management during and after the war in Croatia, highlighting the present profusion of Croatian memorials. She describes the different periods[14] the city of Vukovar went through as symbolical colonization and decolonization; a semiological guerrilla 'presenting binary of Croats as heroes and Serbs as the collectively guilty party' (2011, p. 40). A study on tourism development in Vukovar (Naef, 2014) also demonstrates that Croatian war heritage is highly promoted in the local tourism sector. In 2011, the logo of a Croatian veteran's association was represented across the cover of the city's tourist maps, and more than half of the landmarks highlighted therein were related to the last war, including memorials, museums and war-destroyed sites. Moreover, the *Ovčara* Memorial Centre and the Museum *Vukovar Hospital 1991* were, at the time, the most visited sites by far.

This has to do with the history of the place, but also with its symbolic dimension. In the 2000s, Croats from all over the country would come to visit these monuments and the place itself, which holds great importance in the national narrative (Baillie, 2011). If the tourism demography is now shifting towards an increase in international visitors and a decrease in nationals (Naef, 2014), the war still dominates tourism representations and underlying narratives; this dynamic can nevertheless be called into question. For the local president of the SDSS,[15] tourism cannot be limited to war heritage:

> I have the impression that only a few cruise ships embark and spend just a little time here. It is a matter of marketing. It is in our hands to do more, to keep the people here and make them spend time here. Marketing is not only the war and the things related with the war. There must

be some other things that people like to see. And we know that there are things to be shown. (personal communication, 24.08.2011)

Moreover, the director of the Croatian Conservation Centre points out in 2011 that the mayor of Vukovar at the time clearly expressed his wish to reconstruct the city as soon as possible in order to present another image than that of a ruin:

> There are a lot of tourists coming from cruise ships on the Danube. They get off the boat to visit the damages of Vukovar. The mayor suggested: 'We should renovate the city quickly, so those tourists stop to see a destroyed city.'

In this Eastern town of Croatia, between preservation of the ruins and the whole reconstruction of the city, different memorial conceptions are at stake, which is often a source of conflict.

The tourism sector also actively contributes to diffusing the image of a martyred city, often associating the place with sacrifice. In 2011, a website managed by the Croatian tourism board explicitly put Vukovar in perspective with notions like bravery, heroism and the sacred:

> Vukovar is today regarded as the symbol of Croatian resistance, an invincible heroic town, and also a symbol of peace, reflecting the bravery of its defenders. It was the selfless sacrifice of Vukovar's defenders that gained it its sacred status in the fight for Croatian independence.[16]

On a more local scale, Vukovar's tourism office offers its visitors a promotion brochure describing the city with different themes like history, architecture and nature. One full page is dedicated to the sites of memory attached to the last war, where pictures illustrate a poem to the town's glory and pride: 'Vukovar is a miraculous town … Vukovar is pride … Vukovar is defiance … It is a tear in one's eye, sorrow at one's heart … And smile on one's lips … Vukovar is both past and future.' The last page of the booklet represents a Croatian flag floating at the rear of a boat. Finally, a water tower in ruins (Figure 1) is also highly utilized in tourism promotion and the local tourism office's website presents it as a symbol of victory, as well as one of pain and suffering: 'The water tower will not be renewed in its original function, but it will become the memorial area which will be a reminder of pain and suffering that Vukovar endured'.[17]

In Sarajevo, several museums and memorials are related to the last war and an increasing number of tourist guides are proposing 'war tours' in the city and its surroundings (Naef, 2014). However, Sarajevo's memorialscape can hardly be compared to that of Vukovar. First of all, the Bosnian capital represents one of the main urban centres in the region; it is thus considerably more populated and cultural tourism resources are more diverse. Moreover, Sarajevo has long been considered a cultural epicentre in the former Yugoslavia, and if several state institutions recently shut down or are very close to bankruptcy, an intense cultural dynamism still remains, illustrated by numerous festivals and diverse unofficial initiatives. Furthermore, various tour operators propose thematic tours of the city focusing on religion, gastronomy or general history. Yet the fact remains that, 20 years after the siege, 'war tours' are the most demanded and promoted, according to most guides and tour operators. (Naef, 2014)

The museum scene is also varied, and if several institutions focus on war heritage from the most recent conflict, their interpretations are far from homogenous. Considering those sites of memory associated with the martyred city conception, the *Alija Izetbegović*

Figure 1. The water tower in Vukovar.

Museum is certainly worthy of interest. This museum dedicated to the first president of Bosnia was founded in 2007 and became independent in 2012. Its management is closely connected to the nearby *Kovači Martyrs cemetery* where Izetbegović is buried. An important memorial project was implemented in the area, involving a wall of names and an exhibition on the Bosnian war, following the recent construction of an auditorium.

This museum is generally presented as an illustration of Izetbegović's inclusive and open conception of politics and, more generally speaking, of the broad multicultural image promoted by the Sarajevo tourism sector (Makas, 2012). However, a close examination of the museum narratives shows a clear designation of the victims and the perpetrators. The enemy is the Serb, often portrayed as a 'chetnik',[18] 'a genocide threat' and even as an 'aggressor motivated by Nazi-style propaganda'. On the other hand, quotes of famous figures regarding Izetbegović are also reproduced; one mentions that his 'supporters would become his fanatic followers'. Furthermore, the museum narratives suggest without ambiguity that Bosnia won the moral war: 'We are the moral winner! There are no military victors. We have both won and lost.'[19]

Resisting the martyredscape

Mladen Miljanović, a local sculptor representing Bosnia at the 2013 Venice Biennale, speaks about 'socio-pathetic art' when referring to the constant exploitation of war heritage in Bosnian art practices over the past fifteen years. In opposition, he proposes his *Garden of Delights* in order to paint Bosnia as 'something good, something that one wants to discover, to taste'.[20] This is a mechanism of resistance to the usual dominant symbols of martyrdom or victimhood prevalent in Bosnia.

Similar mechanisms can be identified in Sarajevo memorialscape. In the Museum of History, a permanent exhibition on the siege – *Surrounded Sarajevo* – focuses on the inhabitants, highlighting their ingenuity and creativity. Presenting some of their everyday objects as 'survival tools', the inhabitants, irrespective of their nationalities, are the main actors of this 'living museum': 'Although arranged by the museum's curators, it is the work of all Sarajevans […] With this exhibition, we have tried to avoid giving final judgments, ideological opinions and qualifications. We are leaving them to history, science and time.'[21]

In opposition to martyrdom, such exhibitions emphasize a form of resistance developed by inhabitants, detached from the military context and oriented towards a civilian dimension. This form of resistance can be related to what is sometimes referred to as the 'spirit of Sarajevo' (Volčič, Erjavec, & Peak, 2013, p. 7), or the capacity of its inhabitants to live together despite national, cultural or religious differences. Through the mobilization of 'survival tools' and diverse artistic productions like *Miss Sarajevo*, the organization of the Sarajevo Film Festival or the many plays presented during the siege, it is the whole civilian resistance based on the Sarajevan spirit that is put forward. The Sarajevo Film Festival's first posters exhibited here testify to this particular notion of resistance. The famous 1993 festival poster illustrates the cello player Vedran Smailović, well known for his concerts in destroyed buildings, like the one in the Vijećnica library, thus underlining artists' resistance through cinema and music (Figure 2). In 1994, the festival was organized with the slogan: 'to be or not to be', where the 'not to be' is crossed out and followed by the sentence: 'No question!' (Figure 3) This decontextualized quote from Shakespeare is also now the name of a touristic restaurant in the Old Town.

These examples can be seen as symbols of the Sarajevans' will to escape the war context by pursuing everyday practices and the cultural animation of the city during the siege. If the famous tunnel of Sarajevo allowed citizens to respond to vital needs like food or medicine, such initiatives also symbolize the access to another vital need in besieged Sarajevo: culture. In this context, the *Sarajevo Survival Guide*, a tourist city guidebook parody, describes the Bosnian capital not as a 'victim', but as 'place of experiment' (Fama, 1993).

Volčič et al.'s (2013, p. 7) findings based on interviews with tourism journalists reveal a will to promote this spirit of Sarajevo in order to present the Bosnian capital as an attractive destination:

> These informants in particular recognize Sarajevo as a city that has a specific appeal for tourists, and they frame post-war Sarajevo in a way that makes it a desirable travel destination worthy of tourism, economic attention, and investment. Some emphasize the need to 'market' and 'advertise' this 'spirit of Sarajevo,' an aspiration typical of neoliberal discourse and vocabulary.

Figure 2. Sarajevo film festival poster in 1993.

However, they also highlight tourists' fascination with violence and conflict, illustrating it by the used bullets and mortar available in tourist shops, even mentioning the possibility for visitors to buy victims' shoes. One can see here a paradox in the touristification of war, with the promotion of Sarajevo spirit on the one hand, and a fascination with violence on the other. The latest contributes to producing 'balkanik' representations, described by Torodova (2009) as Western and romanticized conceptions of the region based on violence, primitivism and savagery.

Discussion: living in the 'martyred city'

These case studies illustrate how dynamics specific to tourism can coexist with others, like nation-building and war commemoration. Here, tourism development contributes to transforming places into war symbols and to supporting their 'martyred city' condition.

This process is more obvious in Vukovar, where notions of martyrdom and sacrifice are omnipresent in the tourism narrative and most of the memorialscape is oriented towards the last war. Moreover, tourism is nowadays deeply intertwined with this war heritage, thus contributing to its 'martyred city' condition. This status is strongly reinforced by the fact that Vukovar is considered as an essential element in discourses on the new Croatian national construction; a localized act of destruction evolving into a national symbol.

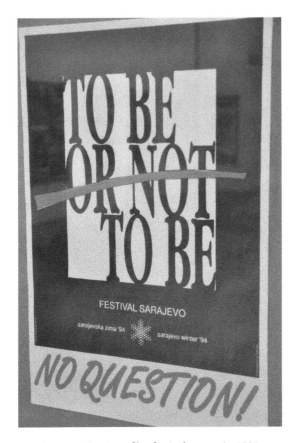

Figure 3. Sarajevo film festival poster in 1994.

Croatian war veteran groups are thus largely involved in tourism structures, strongly influencing the narrative and the general interpretation of this heritage. As a result, one can observe the production of unilateral narratives on war that are dominated by the Croatian community.

Sarajevo certainly presents a more complex case in the 'martyred city' framework. If war memorials are prevalent in the Bosnian capital, they are far from composing the entire city's memorialscape. Furthermore, war museums and 'war tours' are also widespread, but neither do they represent the entire touristic offering of Sarajevo. As previously mentioned, this is linked to the size of the city and its rank as a capital. Sarajevo experiences a more significant cultural and touristic dynamic than does Vukovar, allowing the development of practices and institutions detached from war memory, conceptualized here as resistance mechanisms. However, this does not prevent the Bosnian capital from being characterized by its war image 20 years after the end of the conflict.

If vectors such as cinema or the media are essential to the construction of these representations, the present analysis has shown how tourism can also contribute to the formation of these war images. While alternative tourism sites are proposed, it is still the war that constitutes the major attraction in Sarajevo, partly confirming the United Nations Environmental Programme (UNEP)'s idea that the Balkans represent a place where the '"dark side" often overshadows opportunities based on rich, diverse, natural and human assets, the "bright side"'.[22]

A place like Sarajevo, well known for its cultural dynamism before the war, experiences nowadays the progressive rebirth of heritage elements that are detached from its traumascape or warscape, such as museums, cultural centres, mosques and churches. These elements thus offer cultural and touristic alternatives to the numerous war museums and other sites of memory directly attached to Sarajevo's traumascape. In 2013, the tourism section of the *New York Times* mentioned how the 'creative spirit' of Sarajevo's inhabitants is leading the cultural rebirth of the city:

> The creative spirit that Sarajevans fought to preserve is very much in evidence these days. Neighborhoods, cradled in this valley and ringing the foothills, are fertile entrepreneurial grounds and a testament to the epochs that came before. Cafes, theaters, boutiques and restaurants have sprouted among buildings in myriad styles, including Ottoman, Secessionist, Communist and modern. And locals and visitors alike are rediscovering the surrounding mountains on the slopes that hosted the 1984 Winter Olympic Games.[23]

If this statement should be somehow nuanced given the numerous political and administrative problems occurring in State-driven cultural institutions, Sarajevo remains an important regional centre for culture. In Vukovar, on the other hand, one can also observe the development of alternative cultural projects, but attendance and promotion are very limited compared to war sites, like the *Ovčara* Memorial Centre or the *Vukovar Hospital 1991* museum.

Finally, a close look at issues involved in the interpretation and presentation of war heritage is essential in the 'martyred city' framework. In Sarajevo, narratives and representations can be diverse, as has been partly illustrated with the various perspectives – nationalist and civilian – presented by the *Izetbegović* Museum and the *Surrounded Sarajevo* exhibition. In opposition, Vukovar's sites of memory closely follow the same line of interpretation, emphasizing the resistance and suffering of all the Croats in opposition to the entirety of the local Serbian community, which is considered as the aggressors.

Yet in both cases, one can see a shift from victimhood to martyrdom. This is obvious in Vukovar, where most of the war heritage sites tend to present the entire Croatian community (civilians and defenders) as martyrs, regardless of their actions and affiliations during the war, while Serbs – including those who stayed in the town during the siege to defend it – are considered the enemy. In the *Izetbegović* Museum, this process can also be party observed, but an exhibition like *Surrounded Sarajevo* shows how Sarajevans were able to maintain the cultural life of the city and thus resist in some way their martyr condition.

The 'martyred city' is tributary of the different agendas that determine the political, economic, social and cultural organization of the place. This contribution has demonstrated how tourism and museum sectors can rely on it to develop a specific proposition. Moreover, the touristification and musealization of war heritage can be a powerful tool to attract private and public funding. Finally, from a political perspective, the 'martyred city' is fertile ground for spreading nationalist narratives.

Yet this process is not limited to tourism. Beyond war tours and museums, the 'martyred city' also favours veterans' associations in terms of pensions; artists can be tempted to use this martyrdom image in order to get funding or exposure; many post-Yugoslavian cinematic productions focus on the last wars. These different agendas thus influence the memorial and touristic politics of a place, contributing to the creation of an urban landscape dominated by sadness and pain. Moreover, when the 'martyred city' is characterized by a divided context within different communities previously at war, this process can lead to the reinforcement of war categories.

Inhabitants seem somehow trapped in these 'martyred cities'; a group considered as the perpetrators can fall victim to a memorial embargo, its voice totally silenced. The 'martyred group' can also be held hostage by association with a cause that may not necessarily be its own. Indeed, dying in Vukovar or Sarajevo does not necessarily imply a will to sacrifice oneself for Croatia or Bosnia. This can be even more problematic when victims become part of memorial conflicts and are instrumentalized by political parties, non-governmental organizations or veterans' associations in order to show who suffered the most (e.g. issues involving the counting of victims after a massacre). Furthermore, beyond representations and symbols, the 'martyred city' can have very concrete repercussions, such as constraints and refusals when development projects detached from the war are proposed.

Living, dwelling and interacting in a 'martyred city' can thus be an important issue. The concept of 'museum city' has been introduced to describe urban centres frozen by their heritagisation and toursitification; 'martyred city', in turn, can be described as 'cemetery-cities', reified and frozen in pain, sadness and victimhood.

Conclusion

This last statement may seem extreme. However, the 'martyred city' has to be understood more as a conceptual framework than a material reality; the cities of Vukovar and Sarajevo do not fit that model in the same ways. Moreover, this analysis does not question the idea that memorial practices in general are part of a fundamental process of grieving and giving meaning to a traumatic past. Rather, this concept allows us to highlight some issues and conflicts arising when there is an intense promotion of war heritage, thus contributing to the construction of a landscape that is frozen and tied to the notion of martyrdom. This static conception of memory is highlighted by Nora (1997), who considers his 'lieux de mémoire' as a fixing of time and an immortalization of death.

The main point of this article is to underscore the ways in which the construction and development of numerous sites, objects and practices of memory can contribute to crystalizing and freezing a place around a particular historical event. Some cities are marked by a traumatic past and its intense heritagisation can strongly determine the place's identity, thus contributing to potential memorial tensions. This may lead to the symbolic reproduction of the conflict through tourism, museums and memorials. However, different elements can be considered as resistance mechanisms to this process, and time – in other words, the chronological distance between the current moment and the past event in question – seems to be one of the strongest. Bennett-Farmer (2000, p. 10) suggests this in relation to Oradour, demonstrating the impossibility of fixing time and memory: 'Over time, rain has washed the blackened remains of Oradour.'

Notes

1. Agenzia Fides (2012, June 4). 'The desolation of Homs and the war of information': The words of a Greek-catholic Bishop. *Vatican News*.; Milan Rai (2013, April) Fallujah, city of martyrs. *PeaceNews*.

Info; Fausto Giudice (2015, April 26) 26 April 1937: The tragedy of Guernica. Tlaxcala; Iena Cueto Asín (2012, September 17) Guernica and *Guernica* in British and American Poetry. The Volunteer.

2. The village of Oradour-sur-Glane in France was destroyed in 10 June 1944. The Waffen-SS massacred more than 600 of its inhabitants, including women and children.
3. Luis Antonio Bolín was the director of the National Service of Tourism.
4. Translated from French by the author.
5. Republic of Serbian Krajina.
6. *devoir de mémoire* in French.
7. Translated from the French version by the author.
8. 'Defender' in Croatian. They were mainly composed of soldiers and inhabitants who decided to stay in the town to fight the assailants. They have acquired a valorized status after the war and some of them are now even considered heros by Croats.
9. *Jugoslovenska narodna armija (JNA)*.
10. In Sarajevo, it was transformed into the 'Bosnian Serb Army' soon after the beginning of hostilities.
11. Bosnia-Herzegovina is divided in two entities. The Federation of Bosnia-Herzegovina administrated by Bosniaks and Croats (51% of the territory) and the *Republika Srpska* administrated by Serbs (49% of the territory). The demarcation line also passes through Sarajevo, placing the Eastern part of the Bosnian capital in the *Republika Srpska*.
12. The interviewee is referring to hostages held in Libya in 2011.
13. This ruined water tower is now an important memorial attached to the Croatian War.
14. The siege (August–November 1991), The 'Serb Krajina Vukovar' (1991–1995) and the 'Croatian Vukovar' after the whole reintegration of the Croatian territory (1998-present).
15. Serbian Democratic and Independent Party (*Samostalna demokratska srpska strank*).
16. Croatia at a glance: http://onecroatia.info/en/destinacije/vukovar-2/ (December 2013).
17. Vukovar Tourism Office: http://www.turizamvukovar.hr/index.php?lang=en (December 2013).
18. The Chetnik movement was founded during the Second World War to support the exiled government of Yugoslavia. It was first supported by the Allies who then decided to back up the Partisans of Tito. Some Serbian paramilitaries groups have used this designation during the wars in the nineties.
19. Excerpt from the Izetbegović Museum (Sarajevo, 2011).
20. Rossini, A. (2013, May 17). Bosnia-Herzegovina: The Garden of delights at the Venice Biennale. Osservatorio Balcani e Caucaso.
21. Excerpt from the Historical Museum (Sarajevo, 2011).
22. UNEP (United Nation Environment Program) & GRID (Global Resource Information Data-base) (2007) Balkans. Vital Graphics. Environment without borders. *Zemun*, p. 3.
23. Crevar, A. (2013, October 9) 36 Hours in Sarajevo, Bosnia and Herzegovina. *The New York Times*.

Disclosure statement

No potential conflict of interest was reported by the author.

References

Alneng, V. (2002). 'What the fuck is a Vietnam?': Touristic Phantasms and the Popcolonization of (the) Vietnam (War). *Critique of Anthropology, 22*(4), 461–489.

Assman, A. (2010). The holocaust a global memory? Extensions and limits of a new memory community. In A. Assmann & S. Conrad (Eds.), *Memory in a global age discourses, practices and trajectories* (pp. 97–108). London: Palgrave Macmillan.

Baillie, B. (2011). *The wounded church: War, destruction and reconstruction of Vukovar's religious heritage* (Doctoral dissertation). University of Cambridge.

Baillie, B. (2013). Memorializing the 'martyred city': Negotiating Vukovar's wartime past. In W. Pullan & B. Baillie (Eds.), *Locating urban conflicts. Ethnicity, nationalism and the everyday* (pp. 115–131). New York, NY: Palgrave MacMillan.

Baker, C. (2009). War memory and musical tradition: Commemorating Croatia's homeland war through popular music and rap in Eastern Slavonia. *Journal of Contemporary European Studies, 17*(1), 35–45.

Bennett-Farmer, S. (2000). *Martyred village: Commemorating the 1944 Massacre at Oradour-Sur-Glane*. Berkeley: University of California Press.

Breindersdorfer, F. (2011). *As time goes*. Berlin: Caros Film.

Causević, S. (2008). *Post-conflict tourism development in Bosnia and Herzegovina: The concept of phoenix tourism* (Doctoral dissertation). University of Strathclyde.

Doss, E. (2010). *Memorial Mania. Public feeling in America*. Chicago, IL: The University of Chicago Press.

FAMA. (1993). *The Sarajevo survival guide*. Sarajevo: FAMA.

Höpken, W. (2007). Between civic identity and nationalism. In Sabrina P. Ramet & D. Matić (Eds.), *Democratic transition in Croatia: Value transformation, education and media* (pp. 193–223). Austin: Texas University Press.

Kardov, K. (2007). Remember Vukovar. Memory, sense of place, and the national tradition in Croatia. In Sabrina P. Ramet & D. Matić (Eds.), *Democratic transition in Croatia: Value transformation, education and media* (pp. 63–88). Austin: Texas University Press.

Makas, E. (2012). *Museums and the history and identity of Sarajevo*. Paper presented at the Cities and Societies in Comparative Perspectives, Prague.

Margolin, J.-L. (2007). L'Histoire brouillée. Musées et mémoriaux du génocide Cambodgien [Blurred history. The Cambodian genocide museums and memorials]. *Gradhiva, 5*, 84–95.

Moynagh, M. (2008). *Political tourism and its texts*. Toronto: University of Toronto Press.

Naef, P. (2012). 1991–2011: Traces iconographiques des 'Guerres Balkaniques' [1991–2001: iconographic traces of the 'Balkan wars']. *Revue de la Société Suisse d'Ethnologie, 17*, 28–47.

Naef, P. (2013). "Souvenirs" de Vukovar : Tourisme et mémoire dans l'espace post-yougoslave. ['Souvenirs from Vukovar : Tourism and memory in the post-Yugoslav space]. *via@ Revue internationale interdisciplinaire de tourisme, 2*. Retrieved from: http://www.viatourismreview.net/Article19.php

Naef, P. (2014). *Guerre, tourisme et mémoire dans l'espace post-Yougoslave: la construction de la 'ville-martyre'* [War, tourism and memory in the post-Yugoslav space: Building the 'martyred city'] (Doctoral dissertation). University of Geneva.

Najbar-Agičić, M., & Agičić, D. (2007). The use and misuse of history teaching in 1990s Croatia. In Sabrina P. Ramet & D. Matić (Eds.), *Democratic transition in Croatia: Value transformation, education and media* (pp. 163–192). Austin: Texas University Press.

Neil, W. J. V. (2001). Marketing the urban experience: Reflections on the place of fear in the promotional strategies of Belfast, Detroit and Berlin. *Urban Studies, 38*(5–6), 815–828.

Nora, P. (1997). *Entre mémoire et Histoire. La problématique des lieux. [Between memory and history. The problematic of places]*. Paris: Gallimard.

Oliver-Smith, A. (1986). *The martyred city: Death and rebirth in the Andes*. Albuquerque: University of New Mexico Press.

Pretes, M. (2003). Tourism and nationalism. *Annals of Tourism Research, 30*(1), 125–142.

Riaño-Alcalá, P. (2006). *Dwellers of memory. Youth and violence in Medellin, Colombia*. New Brunswick, NJ: Transaction Publishers.

Rodriguez, M. C. (2014, September). *Le 'tourisme des champs de bataille' au 20ème siècle ['Battlefield tourism' in the 20th century]*. Paper presented at the meeting 'Remembering in a Globalizing World: The Play and interplay of tourism, memory and place'. Le Chambon sur Lignon (France).

Sepic, L., Biondic, L., & Delic, A. (2005, September). *Housing reconstruction of war damaged towns and villages in eastern Croatia*. Paper presented at the World Congress on Housing. Transforming Housing Environments through Design, Pretoria.

Sion, B. (2008). *Absent bodies, uncertain memorials: Performing memory in Berlin and Buenos Aires* (Doctoral dissertation). University of New York.

Topol, J. (2012). *L'atelier du Diable*. Lausanne: Noir sur Blanc.

Torodova, M. (2009). *Imagining the Balkan*. New York, NY: Oxford University Press.

Viejo-Rose, D. (2011). Destruction and reconstruction of heritage: Impacts on memory and identity. In H. Anheier & I. Raj (Eds.), *Heritage, memory and identity* (pp. 53–69). London: Sage.

Volčič, Z., Erjavec, K., & Peak, M. (2013). Branding post-war Sarajevo. *Journalism Studies, 15*(6), 726–742.

Zulaika, J. (1995). The anthropologist as terrorist. In C. Nordstrom & A. Robben (Eds.), *survival* (pp. 206–222). Berkeley: University of California Press.

Cross-community tourism in Bosnia and Herzegovina: a path to reconciliation?

Emilie Aussems

Institut de sciences politiques Louvain-Europe (ISPOLE), Université Catholique de Louvain (UCLouvain), Louvain-la-Neuve, Belgium

ABSTRACT

Memory tourism converting war heritage into tourist capital appears to emerge quickly after violent conflicts. This war tourism has an ambiguous role. On the one hand, it can contribute to a reconciliation process by appeasing the memories related to the conflictual past. Yet, on the other hand, if the message imparted by a particular site emphasizes hardships and divergent interpretations of the past, it has the potential of reinforcing existing tensions. Given this ambiguity, the objective of this article is to contribute to the still underdeveloped literature on the topic and to add to a better understanding of tourism as a way of fostering reconciliation. More precisely, through the example of Bosnia and Herzegovina, this contribution aims to highlight the scope and limits of memory tourism in the reconciliation process. To answer this question, the work of two NGOs organizing cross-community visits to sites of memory of each group in the conflict is examined. The results suggest that the dividing or reconciling scope of tourism will eventually depend on its interpretation by the individuals concerned; an interpretation itself influenced by host–visitor relationships and the environment in which they take place. Under certain conditions, memory tourism may therefore take an active part in the reconciliation process.

Introduction

Since the end of the war and the signature of the Dayton Peace Agreement (DPA) on the 14th of December 95, Bosnia and Herzegovina (BiH) has had to cope with numerous challenges related to the peace- and state-building processes. Reconciliation, urgently called for by external players such as the European Union, is one of them. Yet, within the country, public life is frequently hampered by nationalist tensions.

Heritagization of war memories is no exception in this context. As will be demonstrated, the images of the past reflected by sites of memory mostly emphasize hardships and divergent interpretations in an attempt to distance the Self from the Other. This has not prevented some initiatives from using these same conflicting images to promote reconciliation between former enemies, namely the Bosnian Serbs, Croats and Muslims. In this regard, a study has been made of the work of two NGOs – the *Centre for Nonviolent Action* (*CNA*) and *Transeuropéennes* – that have organized cross-community visits to places of commemoration of each group.

What are the messages imparted at sites of memory? How do visitors interpret these messages? Do they encourage exacerbation or pacification of existing conflict? These are the some of the major questions addressed in this article. In doing so, this research aims to contribute some empirical evidence to the still underdeveloped literature on 'reconciliation tourism'. The objective is neither to argue that 'reconciliation-through-tourism' is a goal that must be addressed in post-conflict societies, nor that reconciliation itself has to happen. Rather, this article seeks to examine the scope and limits of tourism as an instrument of rapprochement. It suggests that the dividing or reconciling scope of tourism not only depends on the message imparted by a site but also on its interpretation by individuals; an interpretation itself influenced by host–visitor relationships and the environment in which they take place.

Tourism and reconciliation: a review of existing literature

A little history

Tourism's potential to promote peace was acknowledged by the United Nations as early as 1967 when International Tourism Year was launched under the slogan 'Tourism, Passport to Peace'. But it is mainly since the 1980s that the link between tourism and peace has been further investigated, firstly by international institutions and later by academics and scholars.

From this time the belief that tourism is a 'vital force for peace' improving 'mutual understanding' could be found in many international declarations and legislative docu-ments (Higgins-Desbiolles, 2003), and one could witness the early developments of 'Peace through tourism' research. Almost completely rejected in the 1990s, this area of research experienced a renewed interest at the beginning of the 2000s, resulting in new publications (Wintersteiner & Wohlmuther, 2013).

A smaller number of these address the specific question of tourism as a way of fostering reconciliation (e.g. Braithwaite & Lee, 2006; Causevic & Lynch, 2011; Higgins-Desbiolles, 2003; Kelly & Nkabahona, 2010).

Reconciliation: a definition

In order to avoid any source of misunderstanding, it is necessary to define what is meant by reconciliation. Although this concept has received a lot of attention from scholars, especially after the Cold War, it has no common definition. At a basic level, reconciliation can be defined as 'a process through which a society moves from a divided past to a shared future' (Bloomfield, 2003, p. 12). At a more complex level, Rosoux (2009) highlights two interrelated approaches to reconciliation widely accepted among academics: the structural approach and the social-psychological approach. The structural approach, which may be understood as the first stage of the reconciliation process, deals primarily with the issues and interests at stake. Through pragmatic confidence-building measures, such as joint political, economic or cultural projects, it aims to enhance interdependence and cooperation between former adversaries. Achieving a basic level of trust, in turn, facili-tates peaceful coexistence. However, the establishment of a secure environment is not suf-ficient to reach reconciliation. It requires second-stage activities focused on the transformation of relationships, something which comes into play in the social-psychological approach.

At a certain point, the parties must handle the cognitive and emotional aspects of the process of rapprochement and reassess their beliefs and identities. This last step may be related to the work of memory (Rosoux, 2000). Indeed, in intractable conflicts the parties tend to adopt a distancing logic and to develop exclusive and antagonistic memories. The differences to the Other are accentuated, memories of traumatic events are constantly revived while the past of the other group is completely denied. The hatred of the Other is relayed through myths, stereotypes and prejudices. The Self and the Other are opposed in an absolute and permanent way within a framework of relationships that is constructed as a zero-sum game.

As opposed to this overvaluing of the past (Rosoux, 2000), the work of memory takes into consideration the ambiguous nature of the past in order to reach a 'just memory' and restore some mutual trust. In this sense, it initiates a dynamic of rapprochement. Both at the interpersonal and inter-community levels, former enemies work to reshape their contradictory representations of the past into a new integrative memory. Painful memories are appeased while the harmonious past is highlighted. Each side demonstrates a willingness to acknowledge its own responsibility, but also to recognize the sufferings and experiences of the Other.

Although theory requires generalizations, in practice the path towards appeasement of relationships is always case-specific, and what works in one case might be counterproductive in another. Each society willing to return to some kind of normality with former foes follows its own long and never completed reconciliation process.

Tourism and reconciliation: four dimensions

The relationship between tourism and reconciliation has been subject to discussion on an ongoing basis. The belief asserted by some that tourism promotes peace (Higgins-Desbiolles, 2003; Wintersteiner & Wohlmuther, 2013) is often questioned by others who denounce an idealistic rhetoric lacking in empirical evidence (Pratt & Liu, 2015).

Based on the given definition of reconciliation and on academic literature, it appears that tourism may be involved at the two stages of the reconciliation process, respectively highlighted within the structural- and social-psychological approaches. More precisely, tourism's potential to encourage rapprochement (and criticisms of this) can be divided into four dimensions: an economic, an educational, a healing and a leisure dimension.

Mainly dealing with the issues at stake, the economic dimension is certainly the most obvious. As an important economic force, tourism is alleged to serve as a strong political lever in establishing a sustainable peace, before working towards the reconstruction and empowerment of the country. As long as wealth is equally distributed, this can eventually help to eradicate the root-causes of the conflict (Wintersteiner & Wohlmuther, 2013). Some scholars however cast doubts on these benefits. They state for instance that the positive economic potential of tourism may not be attractive enough to counterbalance other interests in maintaining the conflict (Scott, 2012), or may even create new animosity between rivals (Pratt & Liu, 2015; Timothy, 2013). Nevertheless, the profits generated through tourism can constitute strong incentives for states or individuals to coordinate in joint ventures (e.g. Anson, 1999; Braithwaite & Lee, 2006; Kim & Prideaux, 2003).

When these act as confidence-building measures and symbols of rapprochement, this may in turn lead to the second stage of the reconciliation process.

The impacts of tourism on the transformation of relationships can be grouped into three interrelated dimensions: those of education, healing and leisure. Although still widely debated, the educational dimension of tourism is generally recognized among researchers from both tourism and reconciliation fields. Although the opposite has also been demonstrated (Pizam, 1996), the revisited 'contact hypothesis' states that tourism encourages person-to-person contact which, under certain conditions (Etter, 2007; Pizam, 1996), fosters cross-cultural understanding, undermines negative stereotypes and prejudices, and results in an attitudinal change towards the Other (Higgins-Desbiolles, 2003; Var, Ap, & Van Doren, 1994). Furthermore, some tourist initiatives such as peace museums are directly dedicated to the promotion of multiculturalism, tolerance and peace values. Their main objectives are to face one's own responsibility and to teach people why and how atrocities could have happened so that they may never happen again. However, they sometimes fail in their mission, rather reminding people of hardships and violence (Pratt & Liu, 2015).

Less often addressed is what is usually referred to as the healing dimension of tourism, at the centre of this research. Monuments, museums, memorials or peace parks are places and objects created to remember the past, to recognize and pay respect to the victims. If they can ensure a sense of justice, those places can also facilitate symbolic forms of healing, especially by virtue of their ability to 'help concretize a traumatic incident, serving as a focal point in the grieving process (…)' (Hamber, 2003, p. 85). The healing value of these memorial sites can be reinforced through specific ceremonies or rituals associated with these places, which appear to have a therapeutic effect (Braithwaite & Lee, 2006; Hamber, 2003). By visiting such remembrance sites, victims of trauma also have the opportunity to share with people who had similar experiences (Braithwaite & Lee, 2006), which can eventually lead to empathy, emotional enhancement and personal catharsis (Causevic & Lynch, 2011). Contrasting with these findings, other research shows instead that such places of commemoration may on the contrary 'help to keep alive the hatreds of the past, especially where there is an emphasis on "shock values"' (Kelly, 2007, p. 4).

Finally, the leisure dimension, although possibly unexpected, is quite significant. The extreme dramatization or trivialization of very nationalistic narratives attached to some tourist attractions allows visitors to assert their Self-identity through confrontation with the Other, while deactivating conflicts. As a result, the Other is de-demonized, which is a first step towards the normalization of relations (Goeury, 2008; Naef, 2013).

The review of these arguments highlights that there is no common agreement concerning tourism's ability to promote reconciliation. What it suggests in particular is that the relationship between tourism and reconciliation is ambiguous. While some evidence is consistent with the 'reconciliation-through-tourism' argument, other evidence states on the contrary that tourism can reawaken conflicts. It therefore seems more appropriate to conceive of tourism not as a 'vital force for peace' and reconciliation, but as a method that can in some cases and under certain circumstances participate in the rapprochement process between individuals and nations.

Although the term 'reconciliation tourism' is usually referred to by academics dealing with this problematic, it should be qualified: far from asserting the capacity of tourism to actually 'reconcile' divided societies, it rather suggests that tourism may possess an inte-grative and reflective aspect in the sense of the work of memory aforementioned.

Research design

According to Urbain (2003), visiting remembrance sites forms part of this work of memory, required at the second stage of the reconciliation process. Memory tourism appeared for this reason to be a good starting point for analysing tourism as an instrument facilitating the transformation of relationships between former belligerents.

According to Marschall (2012), memory tourism is closely related to heritage tourism. Like the latter, the former commodifies historical sites and artefacts as expressions of col-lective memory, converting them into tourist attractions. However, it considers a more complex interaction between individual and collective memory in tourism (Marschall, 2012) and highlights the role of emotions induced by the commodification of memory (Bartoletti, 2010). If emotions related to both 'positive' and 'negative' events can be part of memory tourism, some scholars place greater importance on the latter, such as Hertzog (2013) who defines it as any practice of development of and attendance to sites associated with wars, violence or a traumatic past. Though absent from these defi-nitions, it is useful to take into consideration the identity dimension associated with this type of tourism which, according to Urbain (2003), is involved in the construction, preser-vation and diffusion of group identity.

BiH was chosen for field research. As explained below, memory tourism converting war heritage into tourist capital is valued there as a symbol of collective identities. It partici-pates in the renegotiation of post-war ethnic identities, strengthening them inwardly and asserting them outwardly (Urbain, 2003). As a result, memory tourism in BiH is mainly intended for foreigners, and possibly for visitors coming from the same community, but not for former adversaries. This is why the latter are at the core of this research. How do visitors from one camp interpret the message imparted by the commemoration sites of the other side? How does it influence the relationships between previously opposing parties?

To address these questions, the work of two NGOs – CNA and *Transeuropéennes* – has been studied.

Concerned by the challenges arising from the end of the Cold War, the violent collapse of ex-Yugoslavia and the first Gulf War, *Transeuropéennes* was founded in 1993 in France to initiate a reflection on issues such as identity, memory and culture. Its work interacts theory with practice, the publication of the review *Transeuropéennes* going hand in hand with action programmes in the Balkans and the Mediterranean peripheries. From 1999 to 2005, it carried out the 'Balkan women for peace' project, gathering women peace activists from the former Yugoslavia and Albania. In 2002, 47 of them came together in a 'Caravan' travelling around this same area for 15 days. They met with several peace activists as well as officials and visited civilian memorials. In doing so, their objectives were

> to engage with one another's reality, to bring to light the truth about the recent wars and the question of responsibility, and to assist one another in their respective struggles against com-munity pressures of every kind; against compartmentalisation. (Glasson Deschaumes & Slapšak, 2003, p. 7)

The women also perceived their action as a way to instigate an alternative to warrior and 'male' discourse about war.

A priori holders of this exact discourse, war veterans are central in *CNA*'s work. This multi-ethnic NGO based in Sarajevo/Belgrade was founded in 1997 in the aftermath of the Bosnian war. Through the promotion of social values such as non-violence and toler-ance, and with a focus on dealing constructively with the past, it aims at building a sustain-able peace throughout ex-Yugoslavia. To achieve its goals, it carries out activities ranging from peace education to publications and video productions. Since 2008, *CNA* has orga-nized visits to civil and military memorials with a core group of 20 ex-combatants coming from all the armies that fought against each other in order to pay respect to all victims and to contribute to reconciliation.

These two NGOs were chosen because although they are different in some respects (e.g. timing; participants; duration of trips), they share strong similarities. Firstly, their objective in conducting interethnic visits to remembrance places of the three ethnic groups is the same: to encourage a more inclusive reading of the past. Secondly, they are the only ones providing a comparable access to data concerning key players otherwise difficult to reach: visitors coming to remembrance sites of opponents.

An outsider perspective was adopted to conduct this research, consisting in the exploratory phase of a wider study on culture and reconciliation. To obtain similar data, public indirect sources were analysed as both NGOs published books and activity reports, produced films and edited websites related to their projects. Beyond a mere description of the course of visits to memorials, these documents provided personal narratives of organizers as well as of participants about these events, like in the book *Balkan women for peace: Itineraries of crossborder activism* (Glasson Deschaumes & Slapšak, 2003) in which the diary kept by G. Glasson Deschaumes during the two weeks of the Caravan stands next to testimonies of all the women who took part to this travel. The empirical findings resulting from a discourse analysis based on these data certainly allow for further reflection on memory tourism's potential to foster reconciliation.

It is worth noting at this point that while tourism is at the core of this article, in the cases at hand this concept can be shocking as it makes reconciliation activities sound like sight-seeing. Participants in the field would definitely not define themselves as tourists, but rather as peace activists. Indeed, although some characteristics of their inter-community trips – overnight stays, visits to 'foreign' places – may stick to the dominant and common sense definition of tourism as an economy- and leisure-oriented industry, this vision is totally separate from the NGOs' perception of their actions. But that does not take into consideration the many forms of tourism that are culturally, politically or other purposes-oriented. Tourism is not only an economic but also a social force impacting on various dimensions of human societies, and sometimes aiming to transform them (Win-tersteiner & Wohlmuther, 2013).

In this perspective, the reluctance to consider the case studies through the lens of tourism fades away: NGOs' cross-community visits can be viewed as a form of culturally and politically motivated tourism since their aim is to bring participants to now 'foreign' places in order to create intercultural encounters and, in doing so, to reach reconciliation.

Research findings

Official context: nationalist memories

Before proceeding with the in-depth analysis of the two case studies, it can be helpful to introduce the official context in which the NGOs' activities take place. Since the end of the war, and despite the peace efforts of international players, BiH has remained fragmented along ethnic lines. As far as reconciliation is concerned, many structurally related initiatives have been undertaken, especially with the implementation of the DPA. However, there are still few achievements regarding the transformation of relationships:

> (…) instead of providing a platform for social inclusion and reconciliation, the Dayton Agreement ghettoized B&H citizens into enclaves of Serbs, Croats and Bosniaks, disabling the country's progress, in a political, economical or socio-cultural context. Positive effects on a process of social reconciliation have not yet been addressed. (Causevic, 2010, p. 55)

Heritage and tourism management in BiH accurately reflects this internal division.

During the Yugoslav wars, historical and cultural heritage suffered massive destruction. Every symbolic representation of the Other's memory was erased in a systematic attempt to destroy him in terms of what formed his identity. The best-known examples of this memoricide are probably those of the burning of the National Library in Sarajevo and the collapse of the Mostar Bridge. If Muslim heritage was the most ill-treated, Catholic and Orthodox monuments were not spared either.

But this heritage destruction was not only directed against the Other's memory. The symbols associated with a common history also bore the cost of the war. Many of the memorials of Titoist Yugoslavia dedicated to Second World War resistance were wrecked. Multi-ethnic towns such as Sarajevo or Vukovar were heavily bombed.

On the whole,

> (…) investigations have shown that over 2700 built heritage properties were demolished wholly or partially, or damaged, during the war of 1992–96. Monuments from the 15th to the 19th centuries suffered the worst destruction, with the urban nuclei of 49 out of 60 historic centres seriously damaged. (Commission to preserve national monuments[9], n.d.)

Owing to the need to restore this damaged heritage to implement a stable peace, this specific issue was addressed in the DPA by creating a Commission to preserve national monuments[*]. As for the other legal powers in the fields of culture and tourism, they follow the complex institutional organization inherited from the peace accords. They are decentralized to the federated entities, namely the Brčko District, the Republika Srpska (RS) and the Federation of BiH. Within the latter, 10 cantons have the real responsibility. The state level only has a coordinating role, but to date it has failed to achieve effective harmonization due to a lack of political will. Any cooperation is even more hampered by different legislation within the entities. Additionally, DPA gives no indication concerning the cultural institutions inherited from the Yugoslav era, leaving them without legal status or budget. As a result, the situation in the field of heritage is 'significantly complicated, somewhat paradoxical and rather absurd' (Bebagić, 2014, p. 50).

The main obstacle to the settlement of these issues comes from nationalist parties. Bosnian Serb politicians, in particular, largely refuse to strengthen the state powers or to finance non Serb institutions, arguing it is the responsibility of each entity to preserve its own heritage (Bebagić, 2014).

This political context, combined with a general lack of funding, prevents any effective work for the protection and restoration of damaged heritage. Once again, monuments embodying common memories or those of the Other suffer the most. After the war, some monuments or sites have been still further destroyed, such as Makljen Partisan memorial which was dynamited in 2000 and a Muslim memorial in Mostar bombed in 2013. Some other sites are left derelict, such as the series of 'Spomeniks', the aforementioned Titoist monuments commemorating the Second World War. Others, like the National Gallery and the National Museum of BiH, eventually had to close their doors due to a lack of funding. When the funds are available, they are habitually spent on rebuilding monuments of the Self-community. In the RS for instance the money allocated in 2007 for reconstruction was spent on rebuilding Orthodox churches, leaving mosques or Catholic churches aside (Cano, 2008).

Regarding memories of the last war, each community commemorates the victims of its own group only, collectively condemning the Other as the aggressor. Meanwhile, the victims of the other side are denied, as Self-victimization generally goes together with a relativization of the community's own crimes. For example, although war crimes were committed in the cities of Foča, Bugojno and Konjic against Muslim, Croat and Serb victims respectively, no official monument was erected in their memory.

Similarly, only heroes of the Self-community are honoured. A striking example of this is the memorial plaque dedicated to the war criminal Ratko Mladić erected in May 2014 in the Eastern part of Sarajevo, a hill where the Bosnian Serb army conducted the siege of the city.

Such heritagization of competing ethnic memories at the expense of any common memory mirrors the widespread internal tensions within the country. Heroes and victims, whether human or monumental, are re-appropriated in the name of national projects. It is only when it comes to meeting international requirements that it is sometimes otherwise, as exemplified by the rebuilding of the Mostar Bridge carried out under the pretext of reconciliation.

A safe environment

Calling for appeasement is not an easy task in this exclusive culture of remembrance. The political sphere is dominated by nationalist debates that leave little room for rapprochement at the collective level. The prospects appear more favourable in terms of interpersonal reconciliation. However, this is not without obstacles, both external and internal, as exemplified by *Transeuropéennes* and *CNA'* experiences.

Outside the group, it is often frowned upon for former opponents to visit places of commemoration of the other camp. Many examples show that those who do it anyway are exposed to community pressures, from both politicians and their fellows. They are regularly accused of betrayal. Barriers are raised in their way to hinder their actions.

> It happened that planned event with 20 participants, gets cancelled one day before, due to received threats by the partnering veterans association, directed towards visitors. (Centre for Nonviolent Action [CNA], 2012, p. 50)

Inside the group, the lack of a safe environment between participants is also a problem to overcome. War traumas have generated fears and prejudices against members of the other communities. These feelings have to be dealt with in order to build the mutual trust, tolerance, respect and empathy necessary for open discussions within the groups.

> In 1992, I lost my husband who was killed by Arkan's men on the Ljubovski bridge (Bratunac). Ever since then, I felt a revulsion towards everything on the other side of the River Drina. (Advija cited in Glasson Deschaumes & Slapšak, 2003, p. 271)

Last but not least, emotions are usually pointed to as a difficulty. To run counter to their own community and social environment, to confront their fears and prejudices, to recount their wartime experiences, and also to hear others' tragic accounts of war appear to be a demanding experience for many participants.

> Someone has to hear the stories full of the dead, the wounded, someone has to hear the traumatic stories of beatings from the prison camps. Sometimes I am reluctant to go on these meetings of reconciliation, because I want to protect myself from difficult emotions, and because with the years you become closed off and insensitive to another's suffering. (Šehić, 2014)

The dominant line of thought and personal resistance regularly get the better of volunteers who are, therefore, few in number. But for those who decide to cope with these obstacles, inter-community visits to sites of memory may lead to some form of reconciliation, provided the existence of a safe environment.

NGOs act here as mediators between individuals and groups and are careful to establish the right conditions to generate a positive change of attitude; conditions consistent with those highlighted by Pizam, Natan, and Arie (2000, p. 399): equal status within interaction situations, sanction from 'authority', cooperation in the pursuit of common goals, voluntary and intimate contact, and initial intergroup attitudes that are not extremely negative. Going one step further, the last two conditions appear to be more crucial (Etter, 2007; Griffiths & Sharpley, 2012): based on the cases studied, it can be assumed that the voluntary nature of encounters is facilitated by initial open and empathetic attitudes from both sides towards the other, which in turn enables appeasement of relationships.

Healing dimension

Although connected to each other, the impacts of memory tourism on individual reconciliation can be divided into two categories, those among hosts and those among visitors. Like in Causevic and Lynch (2009), the host–visitor relationships observed in this article are understood as a social phenomenon, rather than as a commercial transaction.

In BiH, historical events often receive contradicting interpretations from the different camps, leading to memory conflicts. When they are not simply portrayed as a lie, the story of the enemy and its sufferings are frequently questioned. Conversely, the visiting of remembrance places by members of the other community may be perceived among the hosts as a sign of recognition and respect: their experience is fully acknowledged rather than relativized.

> On the other hand, a gratefulness could be felt with the hosts, the veterans from the Serb associations, because the 'others' paid respect to the victims of their people and in that

way 'admitted' that the crime had really occurred, without the so-called relativization. (Hasan-begović, 2010)

Another step towards integrative relationships is the cathartic effect memory tourism may have on some people, such as former victims. Indeed, during these visits, hosts usually share their experiences related to the site with visitors. These painful stories bring them back to the heart of their war trauma. To 'relive' it while receiving empathy from listeners may in some cases help to free the story-teller from the burden of the past. 'Today I was healed' (Glasson Deschaumes & Slapšak, 2003, p. 209) said a mother from Srebrenica, a member of the Caravan, after they visited the Memorial. This catharsis may also occur among visitors who go to a place where they lost family or friends, in that learning more about what happened to their relatives may help them in their mourning process.

Whether among hosts or visitors, the mutual empathy that emerges from sharing with people who had similar experiences plays an important role for individual reconciliation. Among visitors, listening to the story of the hosts allows them to reach the Other's reality and to better understand the former enemy's experience. It helps them likewise to become aware of the ambiguity of the past and of the existence of multiple valid realities, the same event giving rise to several possible interpretations. The Other – who was not only the aggressor but also a victim – is thereby rehumanized, making it easier to meet each other half way.

> What left the greatest impression was the fact that things that were happening to us had also been happening elsewhere – the loss of dear ones and of a part of your life is the same every-where … We found the strength to cross the boundaries first within ourselves … . (Mirnesa cited in Glasson Deschaumes & Slapšak, 2003, p. 285)

Sharing and confronting these different realities forms part of the search for truth, so closely associated with reconciliation. Indeed, through the exchange of experiences, a more comprehensive image of historical events may emerge. Unknown facts are revealed to visitors. This can lead them to realize that there are victims and perpetrators in all sides, and in turn to question their own narrative. Official stories are supplemented and cor-rected by eyewitness accounts, possibly supported by hard evidence. Provided that these facts – and the meaning attributed to them – are acknowledged by the members of the other group, an intersubjective truth (Rosoux, 2009, p. 556) may emerge that con-tributes to reconciliation.

> Often, when we visit various towns, we evoke memories of a painful past, repressed, but not forgotten. We found out that a detention camp was situated in the vicinity of the motel where we were staying. A war veteran from this town (…) had been detained there with another two dozen or so of his fellow fighters. (…) This is not the first time we encountered taboo places that hide secrets and that are only whispered about among the local community. (Delić, 2014)

Along the same lines, visiting places where their camp committed atrocities induces visi-tors to face the responsibility of their own community in the war. This does not mean that visitors feel guilty in the name of collective responsibility. Rather they realize that their side perpetrated crimes too, which plays a role in the deconstruction of the heroic image of the Self.

> A certain dose of shame could be sensed because of the violence as such. (...) In their final comments an ambivalent feeling was present in which the veterans had the need to justify their 'side in the war', but they also regretted and felt genuine empathy for the suffering of the 'others'. (Hasanbegović, 2010)

Following these observations, it appears that the interpretation of the message delivered by a site is at least as important as, if not more important than, the message itself. Although the official meaning associated with sites of memory in BiH is clearly exclusive, it can be reinterpreted in a more inclusive way if the right conditions are established. One can however wonder what the influence of time is on this rapprochement. Do these activities have a lasting impact on people? This should certainly be further investigated.

Moreover, in the cases studied, tourism acts as a means of going to meet the other group. More precisely, interethnic visits to places of commemoration, as symbolic representations of collective identity, play a specific role in the transformation of relationships. They generate a space for the expression and discussion of different stories relating to the conflictual past, an issue sooner or later addressed in any reconciliation process. Thus cross-community memory tourism mediated by NGOs acts in the same way as support groups which practice storytelling as a method of facing the past and making sense of it with a view to reconciliation, and of dealing with emotions and fostering empathy towards former enemies.

Discrepant statements

As already stated, the path towards reconciliation is case-specific, and this is also true for individuals. The findings of this research should be regarded in the light of this observation. Indeed, although it is worth revealing all the mechanisms at play, they are not shared by all the participants. Most of the time, the women of the Caravan and the war ex-combatants related similar experiences. Yet some had very different perceptions, opposite to the major comments recounting the tolerance, empathy and inclusive memory.

> And what made it even harder was that, as the Caravan went on, I got the impression that most of the other participants had their own views about what actually happened, and when presented with alternative views, would not even try to understand them. Everyone seemed to have their own opinions and would not accept those of anyone else. Intolerance was always present, and participants from all ethnic groups proved unwilling to overcome their own personal borders. Distrust was the order of the day. (Duška cited in Glasson Deschaumes & Slapšak, 2003, p. 278)

As evidenced by these discrepant statements, the creation of a safe environment is not the only explanatory factor in understanding how exclusive narratives can be reinterpreted as more inclusive ones. In accordance with a certain line of thought in reconciliation studies, the differences of interpretations between individuals suggest that reconciliation is an intimately personal process, which may possibly be encouraged and facilitated but never be imposed. The contribution of other fields of research, such as psychology, would be necessary here to understand the factors influencing personal interpretation that are specific to each individual.

A bottom-up process?

Based on this reflection, it appears that tourism may foster interpersonal reconciliation under certain conditions. According to the NGOs, inter-community visits to memorials also have an impact on the collective level, firstly acting as a bottom-up process, and secondly having a multiplying effect. Indeed, despite the prevailing nationalist climate, some officials have shown interest and support for these actions aimed at reconciling divided communities. 'Afterwards, some politicians visited as well' (Fischer & Schroer-Hippel, 2012, p. 11) reported a member of *CNA*. Furthermore, the activities organized by the Caravan and *CNA* received a wide media coverage. While new members joined the core group of *CNA*'s veterans, both NGOs also gained sympathizers and informal members throughout their activities.

> Not only did we complete the journey with a full team, but we acquired informal team members at every stop. We met people – local leaders, NGO activists, elected representatives – who welcomed us with open minds and supported our action sincerely … . (Jehona cited in Glasson Deschaumes & Slapšak, 2003, p. 281)

However these collective impacts should not be overestimated, especially since they cannot effectively be measured. Likewise, it is difficult to isolate the role of tourism in this bottom-up process, which takes part in a larger process encompassing all areas of society and is influenced by far more significant factors such as the national political context.

In addition, it should be remembered that participants in these visits are still very few in number and that, although they received some positive reactions, there were also negative ones. If tourism actually contributes to national reconciliation, this spill-over into high politics still remains to be demonstrated. Especially if one considers that, if not backed at the official level, tourism's potential role in reconciliation is limited (Pratt & Liu, 2015).

A moralizing risk

In their testimonies, some people expressed their desire to make a contribution to peace and to pass on a message of tolerance and reconciliation to their societies and beyond. This can be related to the educational dimension of tourism mentioned above.

> I saw the Caravan as an opportunity to convey to others my personal experience of the region. So that madness would not prevail over sanity. I wanted to show that horrors of the war and sick minds could not mislead me, my fellow citizens and my town. To show that my town is a town of coexistence, tolerance and love, a small enlightened space, which has managed to resist madness with a voice of reason. (Senada cited in Glasson Deschaumes & Slapšak, 2003, p. 291)

If it is not always the case, it is nevertheless interesting to note the moralizing risk that sometimes hides behind such statements. While deconstructing the barriers between the former groups in conflict, new borders can be erected, between a so-called 'courageous minority' working towards reconciliation and those 'hampered in their nationalism' for instance. Linked to this issue, others have spoken of their difficulty in showing their pride in their national identity while conducting peace activities, as if it was part of a dilemma.

Conclusion

Far from what the rhetoric would have one believe, tourism is not inherently peaceful. Rather, it appears more appropriate to conceive of it as an ambiguous factor that can in some cases and under certain circumstances participate in the appeasement of relations between former enemies. A better understanding of 'reconciliation-through-tourism' certainly requires an examination of those conditions.

Firstly, the symbolism associated with a site is crucial in determining the integrative or exclusive scope of tourism. On the one hand, some monuments draw attention to common suffering to prevent wars from ever occurring again. On the other hand, in BiH for instance, heritagization honours the Self-hero and victims, projects ethnic identity and values and reproduces enemy images. The messages communicated by heritagization as well as those who create them need to be studied here in order to apprehend the reconciliation potential of sites of memory.

Secondly, in the case studies, *Transeuropéennes* and *CNA* use tourism as a method of entering into a relationship with the Other and creating intercultural encounters through cross-community visits to places of remembrance. Based on their experiences, it seems possible to conclude that tourism's influence on rapprochement depends on at least two factors, a contextual and an individual one.

Indeed, certain conditions are required to create a secure environment in order to encourage positive attitudinal changes between former adversaries. In particular, the encounters should happen on a voluntary basis between people having an open attitude towards the Other. This in turn facilitates the establishment of a certain degree of trust, an essential element of the first stage of the reconciliation process.

NGOs played a crucial role in mediating this favourable context within which elements highlighted in reconciliation literature – such as empathy, trust, truth, deconstruction of the Self-hero and victim narratives, and rehumanization of the Other – could develop. However one main question arises from this statement: what would be the understanding of visitors coming to commemoration sites of the opponent community in a non-mediated environment?

Moreover, although the environment in which the relationship is established is a determining factor, it is not sufficient to understand the existence of discrepant statements among participants of the same activities. Why did most of them develop empathy and tolerance, while others did not? Hence the importance of analysing participants' (re-) interpretations of the official story told by remembrance sites, and especially their interpretations of the host–visitor relationship and its context. Indeed, beyond the contextual factor, an individual one is also to be taken into consideration, reconciliation seemingly being an intimately personal process.

Case studies have mainly revealed tourism's potential to foster reconciliation at the individual level. As for a spill-over to the collective level, although it seems that these individual actions may influence a bottom-up and multiplying process, it still needs to be fully demonstrated. While some see this as a limit to 'reconciliation-through-tourism', another perspective is to consider that within the complex and never-ending reconciliation process, every step, as incomplete as it may be, is a step forward.

Disclosure statement

No potential conflict of interest was reported by the author.

References

Anson, C. (1999). Planning for peace: The role of tourism in the aftermath of violence. *Journal of Travel Research, 38,* 57–61. doi:10.1177/004728759903800112

Bartoletti, R. (2010). 'Memory tourism' and the commodification of nostalgia. In P. Burns, C. Palmer, & J.-A. Lester (Eds.), *Tourism and visual culture* (Vol. 1, pp. 23–42). Wallingford: CABI.

Bebagić, H. (2014). Heritage policy in Bosnia and Herzegovina and benefits from the Ljubljana process. In G. Rikalović & H. Mikić (Eds.), *Heritage for development in South-East Europe: New visions and perceptions of heritage through the Ljubljana process* (pp. 41–64). Strasbourg: Council of Europe.

Bloomfield, D. (2003). Reconciliation: An Introduction. In D. Bloomfield, T. Barnes, & L. Huyse (Eds.), *Reconciliation after violent conflict: A handbook* (pp. 10–18). Stockholm: International Institute for Democracy and Electoral Assistance.

Braithwaite, D., & Lee, Y.-L. (2006). *Dark tourism, hate and reconciliation: The Sandakan experience.* International institute for peace through tourism. Occasional paper 8. Retrieved from http://www.iipt.org/educators/OccPap08.pdf

Cano, N. (2008). *Bosnie: la destruction du patrimoine religieux en procès* [Bosnia: Destruction of the religious heritage in process]. (J. Dérens, Trans.). Retrieved from http://balkans.courriers.info/article10297.html

Causevic, S. (2010). Tourism which erases borders: An introspection into Bosnia and Herzegovina. In O. Moufakkir & I. Kelly (Eds.), *Tourism, progress and peace* (pp. 48–64). Oxfordshire: CAB International.

Causevic, S., & Lynch, P. (2009). Hospitality as a human phenomenon: Host–guest relationships in a post-conflict setting. *Tourism and Hospitality Planning and Development, 6*(2), 121–132. doi:10.1080/14790530902981498

Causevic, S., & Lynch, P. (2011). Phoenix tourism: Post-conflict tourism role. *Annals of Tourism Research, 38,* 780–800. doi:10.1016/j.annals.2010.12.004

Centre for Nonviolent Action (CNA). (2012). 15th Annual report. Retrieved from http://nenasilje.org/reports/pdf/CNA-AnnualReport2012.pdf

Commission to preserve national monuments®. (n.d). *Catalogue Bosnia and Herzegovina.* Retrieved from http://www.kons.gov.ba/

Delić, A. (2014). *Through uskoplje, from gornji to donji vakuf.* Retrieved from http://nenasilje.org/en/2014/through-uskoplje-from-gornji-to-donji-vakuf/

Etter, D. (2007). *Situational conditions of attitude change within tourism settings. Understanding the mechanics of peace through tourism.* International institute for peace through tourism. Occasional paper 11. Retrieved from http://www.iipt.org/educators/OccPap11.pdf

Fischer, M., & Schroer-Hippel, M. (2012). *Horror always has the same face.* Retrieved from http://nenasilje.org/publikacije/pdf/HorrorAlwaysHasTheSameFace.pdf

Glasson Deschaumes, G., & Slapšak, S. (Eds.). (2003). *Balkan women for peace: Itineraries of crossborder activism.* Paris: Transeuropéennes.

Goeury, D. (2008). "Wagah border": Mise en tourisme d'un rituel nationaliste à la frontière indo-pakistanaise ["Wagah border": A national ritual becomes tourist attraction at the India-Pakistan border]. *Civilisations, 57,* 139–154. Retrieved from http://civilisations.revues.org/1225

Griffiths, I., & Sharpley, R. (2012). Influences of nationalism on tourist-host relationships. *Annals of Tourism Research, 39*(4), 2051–2072. doi:10.1016/j.annals.2012.07.002

Hamber, B. (2003). Healing. In D. Bloomfield, T. Barnes, & L. Huyse (Eds.), *Reconciliation after violent conflict: A handbook* (pp. 77–88). Stockholm: International Institute for Democracy and Electoral Assistance.

Hasanbegović, A. (2010). *Joint visits of war veterans to Derventa and Brod*. Retrieved from http://nenasilje.org/en/2010/joint-visits-of-war-veterans-to-derventa-and-brod/

Hertzog, A. (2013). Quand le tourisme de mémoire bouleverse le travail de mémoire [When memory tourism shakes the work of memory]. *Cahier Espaces, 313*, 52–61. Retrieved from http://www.revue-espaces.com/

Higgins-Desbiolles, F. (2003). Reconciliation tourism: Tourism healing divided societies? *Tourism Recreation Research, 28*(3), 35–44. Retrieved from http://www.cabdirect.org/

Kelly, I. (2007, May). *Reconciliation through tourism*. Paper presented at the 4th IIPT African Conference on Peace through Tourism, Kampala.

Kelly, I., & Nkabahona, A. (2010). Tourism and reconciliation. In O. Moufakkir & I. Kelly (Eds.), *Tourism, progress and peace* (pp. 228–241). Oxfordshire: CAB International.

Kim, S. S., & Prideaux, B. (2003). Tourism, peace, politics and ideology: Impacts of the Mt. Gumgang tour project in the Korean Peninsula. *Tourism Management, 24*, 675–685. doi:10.1016/S0261-5177(03)00047-5

Marschall, S. (2012). Tourism and memory. *Annals of Tourism Research, 39*(4), 2216–2219. doi:10.1016/j.annals.2012.07.001

Naef, P. (2013, February). *Tourisme de mémoire: instrument de paix et/ou de réconciliation* [Memory tourism: Pand/or reconciliation instrument]. Paper presented at the meeting of the asbl® Tourisme *autrement*, Brussels.

Pizam, A. (1996). Does tourism promote peace and understanding between unfriendly nations? In A. Pizam & Y. Mansfeld (Eds.), *Tourism, crime and international security issues* (pp. 262–272). London: John Wiley & Sons.

Pizam, A., Natan, U., & Arie, R. (2000). The intensity of tourist-host social relationship and its effects on satisfaction and change of attitudes: The case of working tourists in Israel. *Tourism Management, 21*, 395–406. doi:10.1016/S0261-5177(99)00085-0

Pratt, S., & Liu, A. (2015). Does tourism really lead to peace? A global view. *International Journal of Tourism Research*. Published online. doi:10.1002/jtr.2035

Rosoux, V. (2000). *Les usages de la mémoire dans les relations internationales* [The uses of memory in international relations]. Brussels: Bruylant.

Rosoux, V. (2009). Reconciliation as a peace-building process: Scope and limits. In J. Bercovitch, V. Kremenyuk, & I. W. Zartman (Eds.), *The sage handbook of conflict resolution* (pp. 543–563). London: Sage.

Scott, J. (2012). Tourism, civil society and peace in Cyprus. *Annals of Tourism Research, 39*, 2114–2132. doi:10.1016/j.annals.2012.07.007

Šehić, F. (2014). *For the immeasurable minority*. Retrieved from http://nenasilje.org/en/2014/for-the-immeasurable-minority/

Timothy, D. J. (2013). Tourism, war and political instability. Territorial and religious perspectives. In R. Butler & W. Suntikul (Eds.), *Tourism and war* (pp. 12–25). London: Routledge.

Urbain, J.-D. (2003). Tourisme de mémoire: Un travail de deuil positif [Memory tourism: A positive grief work]. *Cahier Espaces, 80*, 5–7. Retrieved from http://www.revue-espaces.com/

Var, T., Ap, J., & Van Doren, C. (1994). Tourism and world peace. In W. F. Theobald (Ed.), *Global tourism: The next decade* (pp. 27–39). Oxford: Butterworth-Heinemann.

Wintersteiner, W., & Wohlmuther, C. (2013). Peace sensitive tourism: How tourism can contribute to peace. In C. Wohlmuther & W. Wintersteiner (Eds.), *International handbook on tourism and peace* (pp. 31–60). Klagenfurt: Austria.

Dark heritage tourism and the Sarajevo siege

Marija Kamber[a,b], Theofanis Karafotias[c] and Theodora Tsitoura[a,b]

[a]Heritage Management, University of Kent, Canterbury, UK; [b]Heritage Management, Athens University of Economics and Business, Athens, Greece; [c]Hellenic Ministry of Culture, Directorate of Conservation of Ancient and Modern Monuments, Athens, Greece

ABSTRACT

Sarajevo bears a rich and diverse cultural past, which includes the three distinct periods of the Ottoman occupation (1463–1878), the Austro–Hungarian rule (1878–1914) and the Yugoslav Federation (1945–1989). But the darkest chapter in its long history was about to be written just after Bosnia and Herzegovina was recognized as an independent country in 1992, when the latest war of 1992–1995 unfolded. One of the most distinctive episodes of that war was the siege of Sarajevo. Apart from the open wounds, the Sarajevo siege left behind a painful heritage too. As a matter of course, the goal of this paper is to try to answer some of the crucial questions related to the management of the 1992–1995 war sites in Sarajevo. In our research, we investigate tourists' motives and expectations for visiting these sites as well as to identify crucial issues in managing 'dark tourism/heritage' sites. Moreover, the paper provides an analysis that could be a powerful tool for the different stakeholders to design activities and promote and manage effectively the war-related sites in Sarajevo, depending on the needs and opinion of their public.

Introduction

In the rich past of Sarajevo, which includes the Ottoman Occupation (1463–1878), the Austro–Hungarian Rule (1878–1914) and the Yugoslav Federation (1945–1989) we can find the origins of the diverse cultural character of the city that is still evident in the twenty-first century. The Catholic, Orthodox and Muslim heritage are blended together to form a distinct multicultural urban environment. Still, the sites associated with the latest 1992–1995 war often overshadow this rich diverse heritage of the city. Sites associated with grenades, snipers and massive killings climb higher on the list of visitor preferences than religious places and architectural landmarks.

This paper explores the commercialization of war-connected sites from the heritage management point of view. The project focused on collecting data about how this new heritage was perceived by different stakeholders, and whether they saw these new sites as heritage at all. Do the war-connected sites when visited meet tourists' expectations? Are the needs of the local community taken into consideration? To what extent it is acceptable to promote these sites to tourists? The results presented in this paper will show the attitudes and the point of view of the tourists as the one of the main stakeholders. It is, however, a limited study and, in this respect, opens a number of questions and makes room for further work.

To come up with the intended results, empirical research was undertaken in Sarajevo. The methodology used included participant observation during organized 'war tours' in Sarajevo, interviews with tour guides, locals, policy-makers and questionnaires handed out to tourists visiting war-connected sites. In our research, we tried to find answers for some of the questions related to tourists' motives and expectations as well as identify crucial managerial issues around these sites. We also tried to come up with an analysis that could constitute a powerful tool for the different stakeholders to design activities and promote and manage effectively the war-related sites in Sarajevo, depending on the needs and opinion of their public.

The dark tourism phenomenon

As tourism became massive in the Western world, the need to specify its thematic aspects and tourists' niche markets as a tool for better service and research was revealed. A specific form appeared mainly during the late twentieth–early twenty-first centuries is 'Dark Tourism' (Lennon & Foley, 2000; Seaton & Lennon, 2004). Smith (1996, 1998) pointed that alongside their dark aspect, war-related sites and monuments were 'the largest single category of tourist attractions in the world'; meeting a constant growth in visitors numbers from the beginning of the tourism activity expansion. 'Dark Tourism' means visiting sites or buildings where death, disasters or atrocities took place 'as the act of travel to sites associated with death, suffering and the seemingly macabre' (Stone, 2006) or 'visiting sites or attractions that predate living memory' (Wight, 2006). The phenomenon was mainly observed by Rojek (1993), Rojek and Urry (1997) and Seaton (1996) who used the term 'Thanatourism' to describe it. Also, Tunbridge and Ashworth (1996) used the term 'Heritage of Atrocity'. But, the field's theoretical masterminds are considered to be Lennon and Foley (2000) and Foley and Lennon (1996) who coined the term 'Dark Tourism' and introduced it widely to the public, provoking an intense academic interest and debate.

Ever since, the research on this field has been constant, in order to identify the sites related to that kind of tourism and the origins of the phenomenon, as well as the management implementation on dark sites, which include the interpretation, the visitor's profile and the stakeholder's appreciation (Sharpley & Stone, 2009). Every site has its unique characteristics, and the ways it deals with moral issues related with death and its presentation as well as with the political impact it has on the community. Undoubtedly the dark tourism phenomenon shaped its current form during the modern years, but even though it is considered a relatively new trend, mainly observed from the twentieth century onwards (Lennon & Foley, 2000), some researchers tend to support that its origins are much older. The difference between the first paradigms and current situation is enormous; specifically after the First World War there has been a quality and quantity change in visitors' attitude and state involvement (Lloyd, 1998). One of the main reasons for this alternation is that WWI inaugurated a new era in the world's history where wars were not a local issue any more, or a disaster involving a limited number of countries, but a universal phenomenon that equally affected every person's lives of every nation (Fentress &

Wickham, 1992; Fussell, 1977; Lloyd, 1998). In addition, social observation indicated that the notion of death changed after the nineteenth century. Death, in the contemporary society, is viewed as a social event available to the public and not as a very personal emotion that involves mainly the relatives and friends, who express their own personal grief as an individual human emotion in the way they are experiencing it (Lee, 2004; Tercier, 2005). It is however important to emphasize that modern-day dark tourism does not present death *per se*, but rather represents *certain kinds* of death (Walter, 2009). As Stone (2011) put it 'dark tourism provides an opportunity to contemplate death of the Self through gazing upon the Significant Other Dead'. Deeper critical reflection of dark tourism lies beyond the scope of this paper but the authors have to agree with Sharpley (2005) that 'dark tourism literature remains eclectic and theoretically fragile, raising more questions than it answers'.

A significant 'dark market' appeared in Bosnia and Herzegovina too; after the 1992–1995 war, tourists, who gradually appeared in Sarajevo, showed high interest in sites related to the latest siege. This demand brought new touristic products and new financial and social opportunities. The question we found important to answer in this context is 'What triggered tourists' interest in those sites?' Was it the personal tragedy of Sarajevo's citizens or its constant reproduction through the media, or both?

The suffering and atrocities that took place in Sarajevo spread around the world through the media. Reporters and photographers moved in the besieged city in order to capture with their cameras the cruel images of war and to distribute the latest news. No media was left uninvolved by this tragic situation and many artists were inspired by the human trauma that the siege caused. Some researchers, such as Lennon and Foley (2000) and Sharpley (2009), have connected the mass media influence with the rise in dark tourism; human curiosity on atrocities, increased media interest in places where tragedies take place, and sympathy emotions motivated by artwork, are creating the perfect frame where dark tourism flourishes, like the case of Sarajevo 1992–1995 dark heritage. Marketers, in their turn, use this proximity that the media creates, in order to effectively promote dark sites that tragedies leave behind. Public information consumers and/or rather future travelers established Sarajevo in their minds as a place of cruelty, suffering and mourning long before their possible decision to visit the city. With the images of pain and suffering and the media expansion in everyday life we become accustomed to such situations regarding them as a kind of attraction; events and places are put in travelers' minds long before the decision of traveling to a specific place is made (Lennon & Foley, 2000). Rojek (1993) supports that demand for dark heritage consumption depends on 'the commercial developments of grave sites and sites in which celebrities or large numbers of people have met with sudden and violent death'. Respectively, Lennon and Foley (2000) support that commercialization of traumatic heritage has erased the line between the political–educational significance and remembrance, and touristic production available for consumption. This latter assumption, though, does not seem to meet the Sarajevo dark heritage case study assumptions, as the political boundaries remain extremely strong.

Based on the aforementioned, the power of dark tourism consists mainly of the historical facts, the narrative behind the physical evidence and the visitor's perception on the quality of the place, rather than death as such. (Isaac & Çakmak, 2013). In the case of Sarajevo for example, there are attractions offering emotions and feelings in a more spiritual way, like Sarajevo's Martyr's memorial cemetery Kovači, but there are also sites with absolutely no physical evidence of the history behind the story, like the Sniper Alley. In other cases, secondary stories are an effort to reach visitors' feelings, or to create the appropriate background to help the narrative, but the fact is that dark sites are steadily gaining value and visitors due to their historical significance, rather than the extend of past physical suffering. Most of the times, management is the most important aspect that indicates the longevity of site quality, as there are effective ways to present the site and its historical background, which create additional pleasure to the visitor and add value to the experience. However, in the complex legal and constitutional situation in Bosnia and Herzegovina, heritage professionals face numerous issues in the management of war-related sites in Sarajevo. The next section describes the legal and socio-cultural background, introduces the research methodology and gives answers to why tourists chose to visit dark sites in Sarajevo, how they rate their experience and what are the benefits gained through their visit.

Research settings

Bosnia and Herzegovina was recognized as an independent country in 1992, just before the latest war of 1992–1995 unfolded. This war left behind around 97.000 casualties (Ball, Tabeau, & Verwimp, 2007, p. 3), ruined cities and a country with a complex administrative structure trying to revive from its ashes. Atrocities and massacres have become a part of the local collective memory. One of the most distinctive episodes in the Bosnian war was the siege of Sarajevo. It lasted almost four years (precisely 3 years, 10 months, 3 weeks and 3 days). It is the longest siege of a city in modern history. The siege of Sarajevo was marked with constant reductions in water, food, gas, electricity and medicament supplies. The human toll of the siege was enormous with 11,541 persons having lost their lives, among whom more than 1,500 children. Around 56,000 persons were injured out of whom 1741 were seriously wounded or permanently disabled. In addition, a number of around 100,000 refugees were estimated to have fled Sarajevo. Approximately, some 60% of the residential buildings in the city were destroyed and only 30% of the Sarajevo's present population had lived in the city before the war (Ernst, 2003; Riordan, 2010; United Nations, 1994). The Dayton Agreement, signed in December 1995, brought peace in the country; however, its results remain controversial (Dahlman & ÓTuathail, 2005; Simic, 2009). Today, three major ethnicities co-exist in Sarajevo: the Bosnian Croats (Catholics), Bosnian Serbs (Orthodox) and Bosniaks (Muslims).

Almost 20 years ago, the Dayton Agreement brought peace to Bosnia and Herzegovina, but it pointed strongly to the direction of partition, creating doubts about its future as a united country. Both entities, Federation of Bosnia and Herzegovina (FBiH) and the Republic of Srpska (RS) have their own Parliaments, Governments and laws, and they carry out most of the state functions within their respective territories. In addition, the FBiH is divided into 10 cantons. The Dayton Agreement also established the Office of the High Representative, which has the objective to watch over the implementation of the different aspects of the agreement. The competence of the central government of Bosnia and Herzegovina is limited to several specific matters, such as the monetary policy, foreign policy, customs, foreign trade policy and immigration. The central state institutions are: the Parliament, the Council of Ministers and the Presidency, a collective body of three members representing each ethnic group. All other areas such as education, health, tourism, culture and the media are left to the entities. The decision-making procedures are particularly complex with a possibility open to the politicians from both entities to block the functioning of the central Parliament altogether.

The whole heritage care system in Bosnia and Herzegovina is characterized with overlapping of competences and responsibilities. In addition heritage-related matters are disseminated in a variety of laws. Every entity has its own law on heritage issues; law on Cultural Property in RS (1995, as amended in 2008) and the Law on the Protection and Preservation of the Cultural, Historical and Natural Heritage in the FBiH (1985, as amended in 1987, 1993 and 1994). However, the relevant issues about management and preservation of heritage are scattered across laws on urban/regional planning and land use, protection of nature and the environment, inspections and criminal codes (Musi, 2012, p. 8). In this situation heritage is in the center of disagreements on the base of ethnic preferences, not only among state institutions, but also at the lower administrative levels. The national Commission to Preserve National Monuments, whose decisions are legal and binding, requires the coordination and collaboration on the part of the local institutes and bodies. It is the only body overarching this complicated system of lower level institutions.

In line with the heritage issues, tourism issues are also disseminated across different administrative levels and different laws. There are four administrative levels considered with tourism issues. First, even if there is no Ministry of Tourism at a national level, tourism issues are discussed in the Ministry of Foreign Trade and Economic Relations. Second, there are Ministries of Tourism at the entities level, as well as Tourism Boards. At the cantonal level there are Ministries of Tourism as well as Tourism Boards and finally at the local level we can find local Tourism Boards. From this structure it may seem that tourism is recognized as an important activity while, in reality, almost all coordination and cooperation between these different administrative levels is of no existence, nor there is any kind of any common strategy.

In the context of dark tourism, it is important to emphasize, that even if the numbers of tourists visiting war-connected sites are increasing every year, those sites are not officially promoted by the Tourism Board of Sarajevo, and the whole 'dark market' is run by private tourist agencies. This goes in line with the policies of promoting common heritage (no war related) and natural attractions of the country, and not going back to the war-related issues and reminders. This policy is also supported by locals who we interviewed, who think that Bosnia and Herzegovina has so many non-war-related attractions to offer, and who are somehow amazed with the tourists' interest in war. In the case of Sarajevo it appears that, while tourists want to do remembering, some locals as well as today's official heritage and tourism politics want to forget. The conflict between the need to preserve some war-related sites for future generations and the benefits that tourism brings and on the other hand the need to move on and leave the war behind is evident in Sarajevo, and needs to be researched further.

Taking into account the heritage-related system's structure and the conditions of the shortage of resources and experts able to deal with the cultural catastrophe created by the war, the process of restoration and rebuilding of cultural heritage remains a great challenge. A complicated political situation and a straggling economy bring numerous challenges to the reconciliation and cohabitation among Bosnian ethnicities. Controversies about the nature of the war are constantly present. Nationalist parties are still running the Bosnian political life, constantly using the war in their daily politics.

Along with the destruction of pre-war heritage sites that the war has brought, the reverse process of recognizing 1992–1995 war-related sites as heritage, took place. The reconstruction and managing of these new sites is particularly delicate to the extent that they produce a statement about the conflict itself (Musi, 2012, p. 5). These monuments are created and managed at the entity and/or cantonal level. The national Commission to Preserve National Monuments is primarily focused on reconstructing the heritage destroyed or damaged during the war. Until now the Commission designated 117 monuments in Sarajevo, among which only one is dedicated to the 1992–1995 war directly – Markale market (Commission to Preserve National Monuments).[1] In our research, the focus was on war-related sites recognized by locals and tourists as a new heritage of Sarajevo. This new heritage is delicate in a sense of managing and narrative, but it also brought to Bosnia and Herzegovina a new type of tourism – the dark tourism.

Research methods

In order to record the point of view of tourists visiting the dark sites in Sarajevo, the research method employed was questionnaires. The survey was conducted during July and August 2013 in Sarajevo. A part of the questionnaires was distributed to individual tourists or groups visiting the 'The Tunnel of Hope' in the outskirts of Sarajevo. Another set of questionnaires was distributed by tour guides to their customers joining the 'War Tours' offered by most of Sarajevo's tourist agencies. We collected 150 questionnaires in total.

Although the questionnaire's biggest disadvantage is denial or weakness of answering (Maliaris, 2001, pp. 178–179), low cost and quick results give the ability of collecting and processing a vast amount of information. The first group of questions aimed to explore the visitor's motivation in the choice of dark tourism sites. A Scale of Significance range was used, where the visitors interrogated had to state the level of importance of each motivating factor between 'highly important' and 'extremely unimportant'. In the next group of questions visitors were asked to state what they thought of their experience visiting dark sites in Sarajevo, while part of these questions explore the benefits that visitors may have gained through their visit, such as information on the latest war of 1992–1995, or the values of Peace and Human Rights. This group is accompanied by questions about their previous knowledge acquired before visiting war-connected sites and whether visitors would recommend these sites to others. The questionnaire was completed with questions that outline the visitors' profile according to their reasons for visiting Bosnia and Herzegovina, visitors' interests and further demographic data.

The Likert scale was used in most of the questions where visitors had to state whether they agree or disagree with each statement between 'totally agree' and 'totally disagree'. A Likert Scale Question was also used to find out how visitors rated their overall experience around war-connected sites in Sarajevo. Interviewees had to choose among a range of 'excellent' to 'bad' and had to specify the level of their agreement/disagreement on a five-point symmetric Likert Scale. Symmetrically scaled responses have the same number of positive and negative answers, while the odd number of responses let us provide the interviewees with a neutral response. Likert Scale questions also allow the respondents to declare with higher accuracy their preferences than a simple 'yes' or 'no' (Stathakopoulos, 2005, p. 134–136). Open questions were avoided. Although they have the advantage of not affecting the response of the visitors asked, typically respondents are not willing to waste time to give a comprehensive answer to such open questions (Stathakopoulos, 2005, p. 168–170). The questionnaire includes also some dichotomous questions, as well as multiple choice questions, especially with regard to demographics and questions relating to visitor interests.

The sampling method used was the non-probability sampling technique of Convenience or Accidental Sampling (Aaker, Kmar, Day, & Leone, 2011, p. 350). In this technique members of the population are chosen based on their relative ease of access. Since we cannot know the synthesis of the public of dark sites in Bosnia and Herzegovina it would be impossible to use any other sampling method, based on probability techniques. Although the disadvantage of this method is that the sample chosen may not be indicative of the whole population, this method is ideal when the population of the research is completely unknown. Moreover, taking into consideration that in cases when there are no restrictions concerning the population, such a non-representation of the population is highly impossible. (Dimitriadis & Tzortzakaki, 2010, p. 115; Kolb, 2005, p. 182; Siomkos & Mavros, 2008, p. 391)

Questions and answers were encoded in variables after being processed in the Statistical Package for the Social Sciences software (SPSS 17).

The Sarajevo siege dark heritage

It is observed that in the recent years more and more tourists come to Sarajevo showing high interest in the latest war of 1992–1995, the four-year siege of the city and the sites or public spaces that still bare signs of this war. From 2000 to date there has been an increase of about 240% in incoming tourists to Canton Sarajevo and this boost is highly associated with the visitation of dark sites in the area. A large part of the local tourist industry is designed based on the desires of incoming tourists.

The end of the siege brought curious tourists in Sarajevo. They wanted to see the real, tangible image of what television and newspapers had been broadcasting for more than three years. They were mostly western Europeans probably motivated by the sense of horror amazement, or adventure, who were traveling to the city through organized tours, in order to witness the atrocities of the conflict. Atiyah in The Independent (1999, p. 1) notes: 'At the end of the Bosnian War, bus-loads of morbid visitors were taken into Sarajevo for the thrill of looking at bombed out buildings and of daring to tread in the footsteps of war reporters … '. These discoverers' interest brought new touristic packages and organized trips to sites related with the war, promising for authenticity and excitement (Hawton, 2004; Zimonjic, 2006). Dann (1998, p. 5) quoting from a Newton's article in the Geographical magazine, (1997, p. 37) argues:

> … A Barcelona tour operator, … , had in 1997 organized week-long trips to Sarajevo, in which clients could take in the market place where 68 people died in a mortal attack and enjoy a wartime dinner of emergency rations in a blacked-out city center cellar.

For many years, the growth of a dark heritage market was achieved without any official state support (financial or managerial), neither at a regional level (cantonal), nor at an entities level (FBiH, RS), but just through private agencies and citizens' initiative. It was not until May 2012 that the most popular dark heritage site, the Tunnel of Hope, passed under cantonal control from private ownership, several years later after the first tourists started visiting it. Controversy lies in the fact that the Tunnel is run by Memorial Fund,[2] which is part of the Ministry of Veterans' Issues of Canton Sarajevo, and seen as highly politicized and nationalistically colored.

As Sarajevo counts several wars in its long history (Ottoman period, Austro–Hungarian period, Word Wars I and II, communist era), this study focuses on the dark sites associated with the latest 1992–1995 War. Numerous sites are linked with this war, but for this research we chose to present the most popular/important ones:

- The Library – Old Town Hall: This Austro–Hungarian building of 1894 had served as a library since 1948. During the Sarajevo siege shells destroyed 90% of the library's wealth and almost the entire building.
- The Sarajevo Roses: a series of bombshell marks in the streets of the city, filled with red resin by artists after the war.
- Markale Market: the main open air marketplace in central Sarajevo where a grenade killed 68 people in 1994.
- The Tunnel of Hope: the tunnel that connected the besieged Sarajevo with Bosnian free territories during the siege.
- Sniper Alley: the main wide commercial road of the newer part of Sarajevo, offering enough space to snipers to locate their targets.
- Cemetery Kovači: the cemetery of civilians and soldiers killed during the siege, where also the tomb of the first Bosnian President, Alija Izetbegović is located.
- Mountain Trebević: known from the 1984 Winter Olympics, it was used as a military base, as it offers a clear view of the city.
- Historical Museum: one of the permanent exhibitions in the museum is named 'Besieged Sarajevo', and it offers a story how ordinary people of Sarajevo survived the siege.

These sites are highly popular among visitors as all of the organized 'war tours' offered by the local travel agencies include most of them in their itinerary. Although some of these sites today are heavily used for political propaganda, while others are more commercialized for mass consumption, we will not proceed in a categorization. Our aim was to investigate the 'dark tourism' phenomenon in Sarajevo regardless of the use of each site by nationalistic, military, religious or other civilian parties today.

The Tunnel of Hope seems to be the only site with a management plan for its preservation and its future actions. On the other hand, the Sarajevo Roses are slowly fading away. The Markale Market is completely restored into a modern open air market and only a memorial plaque reminds/informs the visitor of the tragic incident. Sniper's Alley is a vivid central avenue and only a few unrestored buildings still exist. Trebević is mostly visited for its natural beauty and the exploration of the remaining ruins from the war era requires an experienced guide.

Sharpley and Stone (2009, p. 21) categorized the sites of death and suffering on the scale between the darkest and the lightest. In the case of Sarajevo, we consider that war-related sites in the city should be placed at the darkest end of the scale; they form actual sites of death (Miles, 2002), they are of shorter time-scale of the real events (Lennon & Foley, 2000) and of higher political influence (Sharpley & Stone, 2009).

Tourists' motivations, experience and benefits gained

The first part of the analysis provided us with a set of results of descriptive statistics, a quantitatively description of the main features of the data collected. Our sample consisted of 45% men and 55% women. Almost 80% of them were aged between 19 and 35 years. This is indicative of the fact that Bosnia and Herzegovina is a destination for younger rather than elder visitors. Although we had a relatively young population, the majority of the visitors (74%) had at least a bachelor degree. As far as the country of origin is concerned, in the sample of 150 respondents we identified 28 different nationalities. United States and UK citizens occupy the first ranks in visitation with 17% each. Australia comes third with 10% and in the fourth place we find Turkey with 8%.

The majority (87%) of the respondents visited Bosnia and Herzegovina for the first time. They were informed about war-related sites in Sarajevo primarily through travel guides and the internet, but some of them found out about these sites randomly, meaning that before traveling to Sarajevo they had no intention of visiting such places. The primary reasons for traveling to Sarajevo were sightseeing (41%) and the fact that Sarajevo is a new, unknown and probably 'alternative' destination (36%). A smaller percentage of travelers, around 8%, arrived at Sarajevo because of cultural events and festivals, which means that Sarajevo as a tourism destination is not just a 'cheap' and 'alternative' option, but also a city with a diverse cultural background that attracts cultural tourists.

In the motivations part of analysis, we tested the level of 'curiosity', 'guilt', 'enjoy having an intense experience', 'remembrance', 'having a meaningful day out', 'personal connection to death/tragedy sites' and 'educational–historical' motives. Comparing the level of importance of those seven motivations, our analysis showed that the most important one is the 'educational' factor and the need to learn about the recent 'dark' past of Sarajevo. Right after that come the 'remembrance' and 'curiosity'. We notice that still today 'curiosity' is a basic motivating factor for visiting the dark sites in Sarajevo, as it was for the first visitors who arrived in Sarajevo just after the end of the 1992–1995 war (Dann, 1998).

Analyzing the series of benefits that might be promoted within the dark sites in Sarajevo, 78% of respondents agreed that the importance of human rights was the value promoted as well as the importance of 'peace' (89%). 96% stated that they felt sympathy for the tragedy suffered by the people of Sarajevo during the war and 91% stated that they felt the horror of the war acts. Uzzell and Ballantyne (1998) are among those who have pointed out the affective dimension in the interpretation of war. This hot interpretation effect seems to be experienced through 'horror' and 'cruelty' by the visitors. One out of two visitors totally agreed that the information provided during their visit was sufficient. At the question whether visitors fulfilled the obligation to commemorate the victims of Sarajevo, 31.8% of visitors had a neutral attitude, while a significant 33.8% slightly agrees and a 30.4% totally agrees. Taking into consideration that 'guilt' was not a primary motivation for a visit, the relatively high level of agreement to this statement implies a sense of 'obligation', probably caused by the emotional engagement experienced by the visitors, as part of the 'hot interpretation' effect proposed by Uzzell and Ballantyne (1998).

Almost all of our respondents (97.3%) consider the dark sites in Sarajevo as a part of local history and heritage of Bosnia and Herzegovina. They rated the experience of visiting these sites positively and 78.7% of them would definitely recommend visiting these sites to friends and family.

The second part of the analysis provided us with results of inferential analysis which include certain relations between variables, estimations and affirmation or rejection of our hypothesis. Based on the independent sample t-test analysis, we tested the relation between a nominal variable, such as gender, education level and ethnicity/religion with the motivation, experience and benefit variables of the questionnaire. Practically, we tested whether demographic characteristics affected visitors' responses.

Gender seemed to affect only two parameters. It seems that women acquired more knowledge about the recent history of Sarajevo than men, while it seems that during their visit they realized the importance of peace at a higher degree. To check whether the educational level influences the response of visitors we divided the sample in two groups, those having a bachelor degree or higher and those who did not. Respondents who had at least a bachelor degree considered the 'having a meaningful day out' motivation more important than those who did not have university education, while those not having a bachelor degree considered the reason of 'remembrance' more important than those having at least a bachelor degree.

As we did not want to ask the religious beliefs of the visitors directly, we determined their religion based on their nationality and divided the sample in two general categories, visitors from Muslim countries and visitors from non-Muslim countries. As the war-related sites in Sarajevo are strongly associated with the Muslim Community of Bosnia and Herzegovina, we checked the hypothesis that ethnicity/religion would affect the respondents' motivations and experience evaluation of their visit. Concerning the motivation of their visit, the 'educational historical interest' reason seemed to be more important for visitors from non-Muslim countries, while, as it might be expected, 'personal connection to death/ tragedy sites' and 'remembrance' were significantly more important for visitors from majority Muslim countries. Also, this group seemed to think that 'guilt' was a more important reason for them to visit the dark sites than for non-Muslims. This group stated that they already knew enough information about war acts in the city, so in their case information given by tour guides was not sufficient. On the contrary, the visitors from non-Muslim countries mostly agreed that the given information was sufficient. The last variable affected was that Muslim visitors agreed at a higher level with the fact that the dark sites in Sarajevo are part of local history than non-Muslim visitors. Dark sites were perceived in a different way and expectations were fulfilled unevenly, based on the cultural background of the visitors. The fact that different people conceptualize history and space differently cannot be ignored (Ashworth, 1998). This differentiation in perspective of the dark heritage in Sarajevo also signifies that the sites are interpreted toward a formulation of a national identity and the strengthening of political memory (Assamann, 2012) that derives of the ethnic cleansing associated with the Muslim community of Bosnia and Herzegovina.

However, the religious background did not affect the rate of the overall experience of the visit, the benefits gained (such as importance of human rights and peace) or the

Table 1. Cognitive and affective experience of visitors.

Cognitive experience	C1: I learned more about recent history of Sarajevo
	C2: I realized the importance of human rights
	C3: I realized the importance of peace
Affective experience	A1: I felt sympathy for the war tragedy of the people of Sarajevo
	A2: I felt the horror and the cruelty of the war acts
	A3: I carried out the obligation to commemorate victims of Sarajevo

tendency to recommend the dark sites to others. So, although motivations and perception may have varied between the two groups, overall visitation experience did not.

The next part of this analysis attempted to connect the motivations for the visit, with the experience and benefits gained by it. This benefit-based approach concerning tourism understanding in a post-conflict society has been used before to comprehend visitors' motivations for visiting dark sites as well as their on-site experience (Kang et.al. 2011). For the purpose of this analysis we divided the experience variables into two categories (see Table 1):

The motivations of learning and obligation were significantly associated with both cognitive and affective experiences. Specifically, the 'educational–historical' reason for visiting was significantly related to C1, A2 and A3; and remembrance was associated with all of the above cognitive and affective experiences.

On the other hand, the social reasons for visiting such as 'curiosity' and 'meaningful day out' did not show a direct association with those experiences. It is interesting though to observe that those rating the reason of 'having a meaningful day out' as an important one for visiting the war-related sites seem to agree more with the statement 'I had a meaningful day out'. This association indicates that their expectations were successfully met. In an attempt to find out with what experiences this statement is associated, we came up with results that show significant associations between 'I had a meaningful day out' and C1, C3, A2 and A3.

Moving on to the last part of the tourism analysis we investigated which factors influenced the intention of visitors to recommend visiting the war-related sites and which factors affected the rating of the overall experience of the visitors. Our analysis showed that all six categories of cognitive and effective experience have a positive correlation with both variables. This means that the higher the visitors rated their experience and benefits gained by their visit, the more they would intend to recommend visiting the war-related sites and the higher they rated their overall experience of their visit. Moreover, we notice that there is also a positive correlation between the 'overall rating' and 'the information given', that is, the more the visitors were satisfied with the information given, the higher they rated their overall experience.

Conclusion

Dealing with the dark heritage in Bosnia and Herzegovina proved to be a hard task. Dayton Accord failed to provide the intended peace and left the country divided between three different ethnicities, with distinct historical, cultural and religious backgrounds (Dahlman & ÓTuathail, 2005; Simic, 2009). Those ethnicities struggle to legitimize their authority over space and identity within the same geographic boundaries. In Sarajevo it is widely accepted that sites associated with the latest war of 1992–1995 form part of the history and consequently the heritage of the citizens. However, not everyone perceives this heritage in the same way or as common heritage. Collective memory depends on political propaganda, misinterpretation of history and certain individual or group pursuits. As individual memory fades away there is a fear of losing original identities within the formation of a new political agenda (Assamann, 2012). As a consequence of this complex situation, the dark heritage serves as the only physical evidence that can preserve memory alive, prevent history of being re-written and pass it on to the future generations. This dark heritage has to be protected, conserved, restored and not neglected.

Nonetheless, conservation and protection in Bosnia and Herzegovina is not in line with the international heritage doctrine that points to the nation-state as the main carrier of collective cultural memory and identity. Present approaches are focused on a national cultural policy that constructs identities by creating meanings about 'the nation', through stories, images, historical events, national symbols or shared experiences. However, in the case of Bosnia and Herzegovina, where group identification arises at different levels this approach cannot be implemented. The urgency to preserve the 1992–1995 sites shows that the Bosnian complex heritage management system, with the decentralized institutions, could be a good option as well, when the need to act promptly and effectively is present.

The Dayton agreement left a gap in the tourism management sector, too, (Causevic & Lynch, 2013) depriving the country from a legislation that could handle tourism at a national level and formulate a long-term strategy. Tourism not only boosts economic benefits but also promotes social balance and brings communities together through communication, education, co-operation and conflict management (Aas, Ladkin, & Fletcher, 2005; Causevic & Lynch, 2013; Galtung, 1996; Hampton, 2005; Poria & Ashworth, 2009). Tourism is the vehicle to social exchange and provides great opportunities in eliminating conflict and prejudice by reducing the gap between 'us' and 'them' while we learn to accept the history of others (Goulding & Domic, 2009). Taking into consideration that tourism in Sarajevo has shown a significant increase during the last years, it would be a failure not to pursue tourism toward this direction. Of course, since in a post-conflict society where the dark landscape becomes a symbol of the painful past, it is imperative to implicate all various groups in the process of identification and interpretation of a dissonant heritage (Novelli, Morgan, & Nibigira, 2012). In addition to that, the remembrance of warfare cannot be kept separate and distant from the rest of the social practices of Sarajevo (Alneng, 2002; Chhabra, 2012). Dark tourism can form part of a broader narrative that runs through the history of Bosnia and Herzegovina, including all the ethnicities and cultural diversities that have lived on the same land for such a long period.

We are positive that all the information gathered in this research could be a powerful tool for those managing the dark sites in Sarajevo. In their effort to design activities for the visitors they should take into consideration that visitors' satisfaction and word of mouth are affected by both cognitive benefits gained by their visit and the experience of emotional responses. It is widely accepted by scholars that emotional experiences are important for dark sites visitors and encourage the adoption of hot interpretation, especially in the dark tourism sector (Ballantyne & Uzzell, 1993). According to the findings of this research, in the case of Sarajevo, visitors seem to acknowledge the adoption of the hot interpretation approach and they evaluated it positively. As their experience depends on the interaction with the local community, tourists form an active part in the interpretation of dark heritage. Post-conflict tourism enhances social renewal and should be included in an attempt to promote both reconciliation and social normalization within a traumatic environment (Causevic & Lynch, 2013). Especially in the case of the fragile environment of Bosnia and Herzegovina, where the balance among ownership, power and interpretation becomes extremely challenging issues, heritage should be managed with absolute responsibility, since the multiple outcomes of the combination between tourism and culture can represent a strong mechanism for social stability.

Notes

1. We can also see City Hall as a war-related site, but this building was a first category monument also before the 1992–1995 war.
2. Fund of Canton Sarajevo for the protection and maintenance of cemeteries of Shahids and killed veterans, memorial centers and monuments of the victims of genocide.

Disclosure statement

No potential conflict of interest was reported by the authors.

References

Aaker, D., Kmar, V., Day, G., & Leone, R. (2011). *Marketing research* (10th ed). Danvers, MA: John Wiley.

Aas, C., Ladkin, A., & Fletcher, J. (2005). Stakeholder collaboration and heritage management. *Annals of Tourism Research, 32*(1), 28–48. doi:10.1016/j.annals.2004.04.005

Alneng, V. (2002). What the fuck is a Vietnam? – Touristic phantasms and the popcolonization of (the) Vietnam (war). *Critique of Anthropology, 22*(4), 461–489. doi:10.1177/0308275X020220040501

Ashworth, G. (1998). Heritage, identity and interpreting a European sense of place. In D. Uzzell & R. Ballantyne (Eds.), *Contemporary issues in heritage and environmental interpretation* (pp. 112–132). London: The Stationary Office.

Assamann, A. (2012). *Re-framing memory. Between individual and collective forms of constructing the past.* In K. Tilmans, F. Van Vree, & J. Winter (Eds.), *Performing the past. Memory, history and identity in modern Europe* (pp. 35–50). Amsterdam: Amsterdam University Press.

Atiyah, J. (1999, June 6). After the peace deals are signed, the Gawpers arrive. But post – war tourism also has something to be said for it. *The Independent*. Retrieved November 22, 2013 from http://www.independent.co.uk/travel/after-the-peace-deals-are-signed-the-gawpers-arrive-but-postwar-tourism-also-has-something-to-be-said-for-it-1098379.html#

Ball, P., Tabeau, E., & Verwimp, P. (2007). *The Bosnian book of dead: Assessment of the database (full report).* Brighton: Households in Conflict Network.

Ballantyne, R., & Uzzell, D. (1993). Viewpoint: Environmental mediation and hot interpretation: A case study of district six, Cape Town. *The Journal of Environmental Education, 24*(3), 4–7. doi:10.1080/00958964.1993.9943496

Causevic, S., & Lynch, P. (2013). Political (in)stability and its influence on tourism development. *Tourism Management, 34*, 145–157. doi:10.1016/j.tourman.2012.04.006

Chhabra, D. (2012). A present centered dissonant heritage management model. *Annals of Tourism Research, 39*(3), 1701–1705. doi:10.1016/j.annals.2012.03.001

Dahlman, C. T., & ÓTuathail, G. (2005). The legacy ethnic cleansing: The international community and the returns process in post-Dayton Bosnia-Herzegovina. *Political Geography, 24*(5), 569–599. doi:10.1016/j.polgeo.2005.01.007

Dann, G. M. S. (1998). The dark side of tourism. *Etudes et Raports Centre International de Recherches et d'Etudes Touristiques, Aix-en-Provence, serie L, 14*, 1–31.

Dimitriadis, S., & Tzortzakaki, A. (2010). *Μάρκετινγκ. Αρχές – Στρατηγική – Εφαρμογές [Marketing: prin-ciples – strategy – applications]*. Athens: Rosili.

Ernst, J. Z. (2003). Sarajevo paradox: Survival throughout history and life after the Balkan war. *East Central European Center*, 6(3), USA: Columbia University.

Fentress, J., & Wickham, C. (1992). *Social memory: New perspectives on the past*. Oxford: Blackwell.

Foley, M., & Lennon, J. J. (1996). JFK and dark tourism: A fascination with assassination. *International Journal of Heritage Studies*, 2(4), 198–211. doi:10.1080/13527259608722175

Fussell, P. (1977). *The great war and modern memory*. New York: Oxford University Press.

Galtung, J. (1996). *Peace by peaceful means: Peace and conflict, development and civilization*. International Peace Research Institute, Oslo (PRIO): SAGE.

Goulding, C., & Domic, D. (2009). Heritage, identity and ideological manipulation: The case of Croatia. *Annals of Tourism Research*, 36(1), 85–102. doi:10.1016/j.annals.2008.10.004

Hampton, M. (2005). Heritage, local communities and Economic development. *Annals of Tourism Research*, 32(3), 735–759. doi:10.1016/j.annals.2004.10.010

Hawton, N. (2004, June 11). Tourists flock to Bosnia war tours. *BBC News*. Retrieved November 26, 2013 from http://news.bbc.co.uk/2/hi/europe/3797549.stm

Isaac, R. K., & Çakmak, E. (2013). Understanding visitor's motivation at sites of death and disaster: The case of former transit camp Westerbork, the Netherlands. *Current Issues in Tourism*, 17(2), 164–179. doi:10.1080/13683500.2013.776021

Kang, E. J., Scott, N., Lee, T. J., & Ballantyne, R. (2011). Benefits of visiting a 'dark tourism' site: The case of the Jeju April 3rd Peace Park, Korea. *Tourism Management*, 33(2), 257–265. doi:10.1016/j.tourman.2011.03.004

Kolb, B. (2005). *Marketing for cultural organizations*. London: Thomson Learning.

Lee, R. (2004). Death at the crossroad: From modern to postmortem consciousness. *Illness, Crisis and Loss*, 12(2), 155–170. doi:10.1177/1054137303262214

Lennon, J., & Foley, M. (2000). *Tourism: The attraction of death and disaster*. London: Continuum.

Lloyd, D. (1998). *Battlefield tourism: Pilgrimage and the commemoration of the great war in Britain, Australia and Canada, 1919–1939*. Oxford: Berg.

Maliaris, P. (2001). *Εισαγωγή στο Μάρκετινγκ [Introduction to marketing]* (3rd ed.). Athens: Stamoulis Publications.

Miles, W. F. S. (2002). Auschwitz: Museum interpretation and darker tourism. *Annals of Tourism Research*, 29(4), 1175–1178. doi:10.1016/S0160-7383(02)00054-3

Musi, M. (2012). The international heritage doctrine and the management of heritage in Sarajevo, Bosnia and Herzegovina: The case of the commission to preserve national monuments. *International Journal of Heritage Studies*, 20(1), 54–71. doi:10.1080/13527258.2012.709191

Newton, R. (1997, February). In the line of fire. *The Geographical Magazine*, 36–38.

Novelli, M., Morgan, N., & Nibigira, C. (2012). Tourism in a post-conflict situation of fragility. *Annals of Tourism Research*, 39(3), 1446–1469. doi:10.1016/j.annals.2012.03.003

Poria, Y., & Ashworth, G. (2009). Heritage tourism – Current resource for conflict. *Annals of Tourism Research*, 36(3), 522–525. doi:10.1016/j.annals.2009.03.003

Riordan, K. J. (2010). *Shelling, Sniping and Starvation: The Law of armed conflict and the lessons of the Siege of Sarajevo*. Wellington: Victoria University of Wellington.

Rojek, C. (1993). *Ways of escape*. Basingstoke: MacMillan.

Rojek, C., & Urry, J. (1997). *Touring cultures: Transformations of travel and theory*. London: Routledge.

Seaton, A. (1996). Guided by the dark: From thanatopsis to thanatourism. *International Journal of Heritage Studies*, 2(4), 234–244. doi:10.1080/13527259608722178

Seaton, A., & Lennon, J. (2004). Moral panics, ulterior motives and alterior desires: Thanatourism in the early 21st century. In T. Singh (Ed.), *New horizons in tourism: Strange experiences and stranger practices* (pp. 63–82). Wallingford, CT: CABI.

Sharpley, R. (2005). Travels to the edge of darkness: Towards a typology of dark tourism. In C. Ryan, S. Page, & M. Aicken (Eds.), *Taking tourism to the limits: Issues, concepts and managerial perspectives* (pp. 215–226). London: Elsevier.

Sharpley, R. (2009). Shedding light on dark tourism: An introduction. In R. Sharpley & P. R. Stone (Eds.), *The darker side of travel the theory and practice of dark tourism* (pp. 3–22). Bristol: Channel View Publications.

Sharpley, R., & Stone, P. R. (2009). *The darker side of travel. Theory and practice of dark tourism*. Salisbury: Channel View Publications.

Simic, O. (2009). Remembering, visiting and placing the dead: Law, authority and genocide in Srebrenica. *Law Text Culture, 13*, 292–293. Retrieved December 27, 2013 from http://ro.uow.edu.au/cgi/viewcontent.cgi?article=1138&context=ltc=

Siomkos, G., & Mavros, D. (2008). *Έρευνα αγοράς [Market research]*. Athens: Stamoulis Publications.

Smith, V. L. (1996). War and its tourist attractions. In A. Pizan & Y. Manfeld (Eds.), *Tourism, crime and international security issues* (pp. 247–264). Brisbane: John Wiley.

Smith, V. L. (1998). War and tourism: An American ethnography. *Annals of Tourism Research, 25*(1), 202–227. doi:10.1016/S0160-7383(97)00086-8

Stathakopoulos, V. (2005). *Μέθοδοι Έρευνας Αγοράς [Methodology of market research]*. Athens: Stamoulis Publications.

Stone, P. R. (2006). A dark tourism spectrum: Towards a typology of death and macabre related tourist sites, attractions and exhibitions. *Tourism: An Interdisciplinary International Journal, 54*(2), 145–160. Retrieved from http://works.bepress.com/philip_stone/4

Stone, P. R. (2011). Dark tourism and the cadaveric carnival: Mediating life and death narratives at Gunter von Hagens' body worlds. *Current Issues in Tourism, 14*(7), 685–701. doi:10.1080/13683500.2011.563839

Tercier, J. (2005). *The contemporary deathbed: The ultimate rus*. Basingstoke: Palgrave MacMillan.

Tunbridge, J., & Ashworth, G. (1996). *Dissonant heritage: Managing the past as a resource in conflict*. Chichester: John Wiley.

United Nations. (1994). *Study of the battle and siege of Sarajevo*, Final report of the United Nations Commission of Experts, Annex VI, Volume II. Retrieved December 15, 2013 from http://www.ess.uwe.ac.uk/comexpert/anx/vi01.htm

Uzzell, D., & Ballantyne, R. (1998). Heritage that hurts: Interpretation in a postmodern world. In D. L. Uzzell & R. Ballantyne (Eds.), *Contemporary issues in heritage & environmental interpretation* (pp. 152–171). London: The Stationary Office.

Walter, T. (2009). Dark tourism: Mediating between the dead and the living. In R. Sharpley & P. R. Stone (Eds.), *The darker side of travel: The theory and practice of dark tourism* (pp. 39–55). Bristol: Channel View Publications. (Aspect of Tourism Series).

Wight, A. C. (2006). Philosophical and methodological praxes in dark tourism: Controversy, contention and the evolving paradigm. *Journal of Vacation Marketing, 12*(2), 119–129. Retrieved from http://www.academia.edu/1610347/Philosophical_and_methodological_praxes_in_dark_tourism_Controversy_contention_and_the_evolving_paradigm

Zimonjic, V. (2006, May 2). Sarajevo reveals its war wounds for tourist cash. *The Independent*. Retrieved December 27, 2013 from http://www.independent.co.uk/news/world/europe/sarajevo-revealsits-war-wounds-for-tourist-cash-476409.html

Memorial policies and restoration of Croatian tourism two decades after the war in former Yugoslavia

Fanny Arnaud

Ecole des Hautes Etudes en Sciences Sociales (EHESS)/Institut des Sciences sociales du Politique (ISP), Paris, France

ABSTRACT

Since 2005, tourism in Croatia is growing exponentially, making the country a major tourist destination in Europe. Yet the 1991–1995 war that bloodied the Croatian territory has endangered the tourism sector. On the one hand, the fighting caused the demolition of many infrastructures and the destruction of part of the local architectural heritage. On the other hand, the media coverage of the war and extreme violence of ethnic cleansing campaigns frightened international customers, who fled the destination. Therefore, actors of tourism promotion have worked, since the end of the war to overshadow the conflict by transforming the image of Croatia in the international arena, focusing on its belonging to the Mediterranean area and on the originality of the destination. This marketing strategy has been accompanied by an invisibiliza tion of the war, in places dedicated to tourism in order to promote an idyllic image of the destination. Nevertheless, this concealment is not symptomatic of the place of the memory of war in contemporary Croatian society. Instead, the memory is ubiquitous in the Croatian public space. It participates in the redefinition of the post-Yugoslav national identity and ethnic boundaries, it articulates with the memory of W orld W ar II, and represents a political lever that various political factions and civil society actors are competing for.

Introduction

What present-day tourists associate with Croatia are crystal clear water, rocky coves, wild islands and a typical low-paced Southern European way of life. Since the early 2000s, the country has become a major European tourist destination thanks to sunshine and sea, a favorable geographical position, a rich cultural heritage featuring 'Oriental' and 'Occidental' cultural elements as well as a rich biodiversity. Indeed, the idyllic self-representation and image of Croatia as a tourist destination seem to erase a more contested and troublesome recent past which raises challenging questions about the interplay between memory and tourism.

The Western Balkans have witnessed a ruthless war that led to disintegration of the Yugoslav federation in the 1990s. This war has lastingly affected the stability of the region and altered the social, demographic, political and diplomatic balance between the former constituent Republics of the Yugoslav Federation. The war in former Yugoslavia resulted in considerable human casualties, material, cultural and economic loss. It saw large-scale atrocities against civilian populations and war crimes, some of which are still facing trial in the International Criminal Tribunal for the former Yugoslavia in The Hague.

In a country where tourism constitutes about 20% of GDP, the memory of war is a looming threat to economic interests and stability, which has been particularly weakened by the war and post-conflict reconstruction. It is therefore imperative to remedy.

Consequently guided by the need to reconquer international clientele, tourism stake-holders have implemented an intense and dynamic policy of self-image shaping designed to make foreign customers – which constitute the vast majority of tourists in Croatia – forget the war and its atrocities.

This denial of the war 'situation' raises two main questions: What about the war legacies of the conflict in contemporary Croatian society? And how has tourism been able to bloom on the still hot ashes of the ex-Yugoslavia war? In other words, which factors can explain such a rapid and exponential redevelopment of tourism in Croatia?

This article aims to shed some light on these issues, showing on the one hand the cen-trality of the memory of the war in Croatian society (unlike representations conveyed by advertising), and on the other hand the measures implemented by the tourism sector to regain foreign customers. The logic at work in the tourism sector and the national circle, the divergences opposing these world and similarities uniting them will be discussed.

Methodology

This article is based on data and findings resulting from my thesis in Anthropology: *Approche anthropologique de l'articulation entre tourisme et mémoire en Croatie*. This research aims to investigate how mass tourism and memory of a violent past are conju-gated in the Croatian case. This research is based on three ethnographic surveys con-ducted between June 2011 and June 2015.

In order to study the image of Croatia among foreign customers, especially French cli-entele, I began my investigation by reviewing the tourist documentation designed for the French market (travel brochures, guidebooks, website of the Croatian tourism broad) using textual analysis to highlight the element of culture and history Croatia presents to visitors. I deepened this research by conducting an ethnographic survey on many sites visited by foreign tourists on the Adriatic coast, in order to identify the representations and practices of foreign visitors and also to analyze how the Croatian identity was staged on-the-ground to attract these consumers.

Parallel to this tourism research, I focused on the memory of the 1991–1995 war, study-ing the material realm of memory (monuments, museums, memorials, headstones, ceme-teries, cenotaphs) which dots the territory. I also focused on events dedicated to the 'Homeland War' which punctuate the national calendar and took place during my field-work (commemorative ceremonies, exhibitions, masses), considering these commemora-tive practices as '*Lieux de mémoire idéels*',[1] according to Pierre Nora (see Les lieux de mémoire, 1984, for more details on this concept).

In addition to this multi-sited survey, I undertook a short-term monograph in the cities of Zagreb (capital of Croatia) and Vukovar (emblematic city of the Homeland War) since

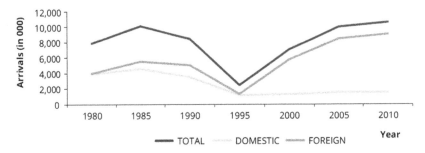

Tourist arrivals 1980 - 2010 (in 000)			
	TOTAL	DOMESTIC	FOREIGN
1980	7,929	3,922	4,007
1985	10,125	4,569	5,556
1990	8,497	3,477	5,020
1995	2,438	1,113	1,324
2000	7,136	1,305	5,831
2005	9,995	1,528	8,467
2010	10,604	1,493	9,111

Figure 1. Tourism arrival 1980–2010.Source: Tourism in figures 2013, p.18.

these two sites are central in the process of memorialization of the war. This ethnographic survey aimed to understand the uses of memory and endogenous representations of war.

During this research I resorted to direct observation, interviews, participant observation as well as inquiry based on the circumstantial paradigm developed by Carlo Ginzburg. Using this approach during my explorations and my daily life in the field, I paid constant and sustained attention to infinitesimal traces and tiny details, considering them as clues to decrypt a reality difficult to access, according to Ginzburg (1980, p. 9), ' … sometimes infinitesimal traces allow to understand a deeper reality, it would be impossible to seize by other means'.[2]

The uses of memory two decades after the war in former Yugoslavia

A large majority of foreign visitors only see Croatia as an idyllic postcard destination and do not have access to the memory of the war, because it has no place in the self-presentation designed for tourists. But it must be noted that the recent past of war has left, social, political, economic, psychological marks that will lastingly influence the daily lives of its inhabitants.

The national calendar is punctuated with commemorative ceremonies and memory exerts considerable influence on social and political Croatian life.

The territory is strongly marketed by the memory of war, either through the scars of fights that dot the landscape or through remembrance places set up as heritage sites.

This is particularly evident in Eastern Slavonia, a region horribly mutilated by war. However, memorialization is notable even in coastal cities where tourism is the main economic activity, as I have noticed during my investigation in Split, Dubrovnik, Zadar and Šibenik. However, in areas devoted to tourism the expression of memory is more discreet and less visible because of its incompatibility with the requirements of mass tourism. We will develop this point further.

The memory of the war as a national narrative of victimization

The memory of the former Yugoslavia war is omnipresent in Croatia and occupies a prominent place in the public space, in the building of the Croatian state and the definition of national identity.

The memory of the war is rooted in both the daily territories and the exceptional space-time and is ritualized in public commemorations. Indeed, the memorial markers are visible in both ordinary and familiar urban landscape (residual traces of conflict through the visible territory, toponyms, commemorative plaques and monuments punctuating the space of the city) and in circumscribed places devoted to memory, whose access implies an active and voluntary process, as displacement or even the payment of an entrance fee, such as museums, memorials, exhibition. Besides this material anchorage in space, memory, as a shared representation of the past implies speeches, practices, transmission channels and protagonists.

The study of the various memorial events (material and immaterial, durable or ephemeral) available during my fieldwork in Croatia allows to expose local memorial standards and collective representations that prevail in Croatia two decades after the conflict. The analysis of these official memorial expressions (temporary or permanent exhibitions, memorials, museums, memorials, monuments, textbooks, etc.) allows to highlight a univocal hegemonic reading of the former Yugoslavia war. In addition to that, decryption of individual practices, observed during my investigation (tags, tattoos, private altars, memorial pilgrimage, etc.) supported by interviews, allows to understand how this reading of the past is embedded and embodied locally.

The memory of the war, as developed currently in Croatia by nationalist political elites ruling almost continuously since the independence, constitutes a national narrative of victimization. Indeed, in this narrative Croatia presents itself as a victim of illegitimate and barbaric Serbian aggression. The war, locally called 'patriotic war' (*Domovinski rat*), is considered as the founding act of an independent and sovereign Croatia, as a just and legitimate defensive war, a struggle for the sovereignty of the State, a fight for the integrity of the Fatherland to face the illegitimate territorial claims of Serbia associated to local Serb forces, planning to build the 'Greater Serbia' – this ethnically homogeneous state fantasized by Slobodan Milosevic. The conflict was characterized by full-scale ethnic cleansing campaigns and provoked a surge of unprecedented violence against populations based on their ethno-national belonging. Therefore, definitions of victim and perpetrator in the memorial narrative are based on the essentialization of ethnicity and reification of identity that prevailed during the war and generate a polarization between 'self/victim' (Croatian) and 'Other/perpetrator' (Serbian).

In this narrative Croatia fashions itself as victim; it is therefore inconceivable to mention Croatian responsibility in the war. Yet despite the efforts of nationalist memory entrepreneurs to endorse this stance of victimhood, a number of facts contradict this version of history. Indeed, Croatia has been part of the atrocious war that has led to the breakup of Yugoslavia. The newly independent Republic actually undertook to protect its population and its cultural heritage against bloodthirsty violence of the Serbian militias operating in its territory. It actually suffered terrible losses and tremendous suffering, and struggled to try to preserve its territorial integrity. However, presenting the Croatian nation as an angelic victim of Serbian barbarism is a falsification of history.

Indeed, Franjo Tudjman, president of Croatia during the conflict, aspired to create an ethnically homogeneous state, a 'Greater Croatia', named *Hrvatska Iseljena*,[3] like his Serbian counterpart Slobodan Milosevic. This project was based on expulsion of non-Croatian minorities, repatriation of Croats from the diaspora and the annexation of Herzegovina (Bosnian region with a significant Croatian population). In fact, ICTY's investigations have demonstrated the use of violence against non-Croat populations by the Croatian armed forces for this purpose. They participated in atrocities against Bosnian populations, prior to ally with the Bosnian forces against the Serbian enemy in Bosnia. During the reconquest of the territory in 1995, Local Serbs, in turn, have been targeted by ethnic cleansing campaigns.

These facts, yet to be proven, are completely passed over in silence; they are absolutely taboo when they are not simply denied, insofar as they contradict the victimhood interpretation of the war.

Also, in the Croatian official memorial narrative, there is no place for the evocation of the Croatian responsibility for the war and the violence inflicted to the 'Other' on the basis ethno-national criteria. It is impossible to mention obstacles implemented by the government to prevent the return of Serbian refugees, while the High Commissioner for refugees denounces such practices. Similarly, it is impossible to mention discriminations based on ethnic criteria that still occur nowadays. Because, as Banjeglav (2015, n.p.) argues 'many in Croatia thought it was impossible for Croatian Army members to have committed war crimes, since the Homeland War was perceived as being defensive, just and liberating'. This victimization narrative implies a focus on its own suffering, its own victims, its own losses, on the trauma that such a war provokes, on the atrocities endured and the violence suffered. This gives rise to a demonization of the 'other', that is, 'Serbian' (with an undifferentiated use of singular and plural forms), latent biologization of ethnic identity and alterity essentialization. The Other, the enemy, is accused of all evils; he is considered to be solely responsible for the atrocities, violence, abuses and even war.

This interpretation of events is not specifically Croat. All parties involved in the conflict use this rhetoric of victimhood which consist in ascribing responsibility for crimes to the enemy, accusing the opponent of barbarism and tracking the number of victims (in order to underestimate its own crimes by a comparison that relativize them). These narratives have many similarities with the antebellum nationalist war-fomenting rhetorics.

Moreover, in the collective memory, the 1991–1995 war is contemplated in its articulation with World War II. Through the genealogy of the conflict and the language used to describe the belligerents, the war appears as a logical, even inevitable consequence of World War II. This interpretation of a contemporary conflict by the yardstick of past dynamics, actors and issues gives the appearance of a continuous and unchanged history, a cyclic repetition of violence, due to the barbarity of the hereditary enemy. I would like to dwell on this point with Rolland-Traina (2011) who reached the same conclusion regarding the memory of the war in Bosnia:

> The interpretation of the conflict in the light of the past is also expressed in the identification of the actors of the present with those of the past. This is reflected by the use of appellations "četniks" and "ustaša" not only by the media at the heart of the conflict and by politicians and intellectuals, but also by ordinary people […] The assimilation of contemporary actors with those from the past results from deliberate instrumentalization and the reactivation of

family memories in the national context. The use of same words to describe differents actors caught in various dynamics and contexts leads to the perception of history as a cyclical time (as the eternal repetition of tragic episodes) more easily because still vivid family memories of the tragedies of the Second World War were ready to be reactivated.[4] (p. 77)

Considering the conflict as a consequence of antediluvian endemic hatreds, as a vicious cycle of retaliation is a rhetoric used to remove the political dimensions of the war. This reasoning allows the denial of any liability in triggering or progress of the conflict, and lends support the victimhood reading. This assimilation of contemporary actors with the past protagonists reactivates family memories still affected by the tragedies of World War II in order to manipulate this amalgam for a political purpose.

Nationalist uses of memory in Croatia

In a country where the political elite – ruling almost continuously since the independence – is ridden by judicial scandals (such as corruption, money misappropriation and secret party funding), the use of powerful emotional levers diverts citizens' attention by exploiting the memory for electoral purposes. Indeed, veterans of the war in former Yugoslavia represent a powerful lobby where each party is trying to gain support from and most families have a personal connection to the war, while the use of memory of the war is an effective political argument. On the other hand, the memory of the war provides an additional resource in the rebuilding of the Croatian national identity, which has been initiated in the late 1980s.

Indeed, the coming to power of the nationalist movement in the former republics of the Yugoslav federation in the 1990s led to the questioning of values and principles at the foundation of collective identities during the socialist era. Political and intellectual elite wanted to replace the Yugoslav principles – considered as obsolete – by the nationalist ideology, in order to found a new imagined community (see Anderson, 2006 for more details on this issue), by distinguishing themselves, both earlier periods of history (especially the Yugoslav socialism) and neighboring nations.

Despite the ideological claim of a millennium-old history, Croatia is a young republic, whose independence is very recent and has been contested by the Yugoslav authorities, causing a violent war. Croatia is looking for recognition and legitimacy, and is seeking to establish its cultural specificity. Therefore, it involves to develop a proper national identity, to create a new mode of social cohesion, to assert its cultural characteristics and distinguish itself from neighboring nations, highlighting its uniqueness compared to the rest of the Balkan Peninsula, by the insistence on the differences to the detriment of similarities (Delaperrière, Lory, & Marès, 2005). In a region marked by great religious diversity and a turbulent past, language, religion and memory are key resources to redefine a national identity and to mark the new boundaries between ingroup and outgroup. As these cultural dimensions have strong cohesive properties, the new procedures of self-definition, required by the change of political regime, therefore involved overinvestment of these cultural markers. The war exacerbated a process that started before the independence. It caused a clenching around these cultural determinants, both in the will of distinction and because ethnic cleansing has targeted civilian populations based on their ethno-national belonging, metamorphosing the entire nation into a 'victim' status.

In their determination to distinguish themselves, nationalist elites have spread cultural stereotypes, making the separation inevitable. Therefore, cohabitation was considered to be an impossible option between Serbians presented as 'patriarchal', 'bellicose', 'oriental' people and Croatians perceived as 'civilized', 'literate', 'mannerly', 'westerner', 'democratic' people (Mac Donald, 2001). The belief in historical, cultural, psychological and even racial irreconcilable differences between Croatian and Serbian legitimized the separatist aspirations of the nationalist leaders.

This explains the importance of language issue in this process of distinction. As MacDonald explains, linguistic differences between the Serbian and Croatian language are instrumentalized and exacerbated because, since the nineteenth century, a separate language is the marker of a separate nation. Therefore, the ambitions of Croatian independence were accompanied by a reform of language in order to purify it of its external influences, implied Serbian influences, to find a pure, authentic, immaculate Croatian language that would legitimize the creation of a sovereign state:

> On the eve of independence, the following opinion prevailed: if it were possible to establish the legitimacy of the Croatian language, the idea of a separate Croatian nation would impose by itself, a nation which through its language would be more peaceful and western than its Yugoslav neighbors. The linguistic reform was designed as part of a set of myths and symbols intended to free the nation from decades of communist plunder and corruption. (Mac Donald, 2001, p. 136)

This 'narcissism of small differences' in the words of Freud (1929) which results in the accentuation of differences and the attenuation of similarities is a classic mechanism of nation-state building. It is frequently observed in tense situations between culturally close border states, such as Croatia and Serbia (Diatkine, 1993; Vigneault, 2012). Language is an appropriate cultural determinant for this kind of instrumentalization, because, according to Goulding and Domic (2008) 'all languages have elements of political self-assertion, which may become exaggerated when attempting to bring about regional secessionism and political independence by linguistic separatism' (p. 97)

The reshaping the Croatian identity has also involved an extensive historiographical revision impelled by the authorities, usually without consultation of historians. This rereading of the past based on present issues is intended to affirm the Croatian statehood and sovereignty and 'to legitimate the new governing institutions, territorial integrity and borders, and a ruling elite that lay claim to the founding myths of the country' (Pavlakovic, 2007).

This rereading of the past mainly concerns World War II and the Yugoslav era. Indeed, the access to power of the Nationalist Party was accompanied by banishment of the communist legacy from the public arena. The social, political and cultural Yugoslav heritage is anathematized. Monuments and architecture of the Tito time undergo sudden de-legitimization for a regime now considered responsible for all ills. This heritage is therefore destroyed during moments of cathartic violence or merely abandoned, at the mercy of nature. The Partisan movement is no longer revered as a liberating force, but reviled for its authoritarianism and discriminatory character. This radical change of perspective is because Titoism is considered in the Croatian nationalist mythology as a synonym for Serbian hegemony, for the subjugation and oppression of Croats. Tito's regime is accused of having created an ideological and biased version of history, using a Marxist interpretation grid of events, while the nationalist historiography presents itself as rational and objective.

Alongside this denigration of Titoism, a past considered as shameful, the Ustası regime of Ante Pavelić, is being rehabilitated. The memory of the Ustası era was marked with the seal of prohibition during the Yugoslav period, but the independence of Croatia liberated speech and led to a reversal of perspective toward that fascist State. The open glorification or apology for this fascist regime is not conceivable in the context of accession to the European Union; however, there are evidences[5] that the Croatian State seeks to clean Ustası's name. The focus on the massacre of members and sympathizers of the regime put to rout by Tito Partisans in the forest Bleiburg in May 1945 allows for a victimhood posture and helps to make an unmentionable past acceptable.

This revision of history according to the precepts of nationalist ideology is conveyed through different political rituals, especially public commemorations. According to Pavlakovic (2007):

> War commemorations are important rituals for a society to remember the dead, grieve for the victims of violence, and honor the soldiers who gave their lives for their country. This is no different in Croatia, which suffered thousands of casualties and widespread destruction in its struggle for independence. But these commemorations also often serve as platforms for politicians to ensure that their version of the past is what gets recorded as history. Moreover, the content of commemorations can serve as a gauge of how a society remembers its past.

Commemorations, but also monuments, museums, media, as well as street names and language and all 'everyday signifiers of the past' (Goulding & Domic, 2008, p. 91), transmit the cosmogony of nationalist elites and their interpretation of the past. According to Goulding and Domic (2008):

> In Croatia the past, history and heritage are closely aligned to the dominant political system and as such the past can also be used as a vehicle to create a greater sense of nationalism and social bounding. However, because the past is gone, it can be tampered with or rewritten in order to legitimize and gain acceptance of political messages and ideologies. In other words, museum and heritage may become cultural carriers of ideology, imbedded in selective version of history. Consequently, heritage can be used as a powerful weapon in support of political rhetoric and ideologies, particularly when used in conjonction with the revival of tradition and, in this case, redundant languages. (p. 99)

By sharing the suffering, it implies the memory of the war is a powerful social cement. It is fundamental in the development of self-representation of the post-Yugoslav Croatian society and reinforces the sense of identity. It represents a legacy to bequeath to future generations, and has a central importance in the collective imagination.

From this network of tangible and intangible sites of memory emanates a sense of shared, unified, consensual memory. Yet, this impression is an illusion, maintained because the memory is a central resource in the formation of the new national identity. The hegemonic nature of the official memory should not hide the existence of divergent narratives and conflicting memories. Even if their expression is very limited and underground, they challenge the official commemorative script. Within the Croatian community, there are dissensions about the memory and its uses. Neither the dominant reading of the war nor the essentialist conception of identity that underpins it can secure the unanimous. Human rights activists, 'yougonostalgiques', 'anti-fascist' activist, members of educated cosmopolitan urban youth or members of associative sector criticize the use of the memory of the war. They protest against the abuses it causes and refuse the ethnic polarization of the categories of victims and perpetrators. These actors convey some competing narratives regarding war and national identity.

Furthermore, the Manichean opposition 'Croatian' vs. 'Serbian' excludes other minorities present in Croatia (Italian, German, Hungarian, Russian, Roma, Jewish, etc.), and all individuals born from 'mixed' families that do not recognize themselves in this essentialist and simplistic portrayal.

Finally, within the Serbian community of Croatia circulates memorial narrative that completely contradicts the official remembrance practices. Indeed, the memorial narrative of the Serbian community is also a narrative of victimization based on ethno-national belonging and the dichotomy Self = victim versus Other = perpetrator. In this case, Croatia as an independent state is presented as an oppressor, continuing ethnic homogenization – started at the end of the war – in silence by means of symbolic violence, practicing in shadow a real ethnocide, and refusing to recognize the crimes, discrimination and abuse suffered by the Serbian before, during and after the war. This narrative is carried by Serbian nationalist representatives, and it is as radical and exclusive as the Croatian version. It emphasizes Serbian victims of the war, the suffering endured in the name of ethnicity and eludes responsibilities and crimes committed by the Serbian side. Local Serbs consider that they are ostracized, that their cultural contribution is denied since the independence of Croatia and their memory banished from the public space circulates only through whispered stories. Therefore, the coexistence of these two memories is a source of severe tensions, which complicate the cohabitation of these two communities two decades after the war, partly because each side believes that it is the exclusive holder of the truth. The community relations are marked by mistrust, resentment or hatred, even if violence rarely erupts. Nevertheless the incompatibility of these memories

Figure 2. Ceremony commemorating the victims of the Homeland War (Split, August 2011).

resulted in vandalization against the Other's monuments, considered as an outrage against the memory of the in-group and against the truth. As Baillie (2012) says about the city of Vukovar, these competitive memorialization practices create symbolic boundaries between ethnic groups within a shared space. So memorialization, erecting insurmountable borders, becomes an obstacle to reconciliation.

War, memory and mass tourism: a fundamental incompatibility

Besides the fact that it represents a real national trauma, due to the wave of violence against the people it has caused, and the magnitude of its human, social and material consequences, 1991–1995's War also represented a serious crisis for the tourism sector (Figure 1).

Indeed, the conflict resulted in a collapse of flows with an 80% drop in tourism traffic due to an equivalent decrease of international arrivals. It must be noted, however, that even in the course of the war, tourism was never completely interrupted, with an average of almost two million tourists per year between 1991 and 1995 (compared to the pre-war level with eight million visitors).

On the one hand, this situation is due to the continuation of domestic tourism on the Adriatic coast. Indeed, the Croatian visitors had a better understanding of the conflict, the theatre of operations and involved risks, and did not have the opportunity to go abroad for their holidays. Therefore, throughout the conflict, even if we note a drastic drop in numbers, tourism persisted in areas which were little or not affected by fighting, namely in Istria and, more marginally, on the Adriatic islands and some resorts in Dalmatia.

Istria remained accessible and safe, even during the war, and its infrastructure was not damaged. This is why, on the other hand, the region continued to receive significant flows of international visitors, encouraged by a dumping strategy implemented in state resorts and national airlines to maintain an activity with a more daring clientele.

Istria, which was not affected by the fighting, is a traditional destination area for visitors from Slovenia, Austria, Hungary and the Czech Republic. They constitute a geographically and historically close clientele with longstanding links to the Adriatic coast.

This clientele has a good knowledge of the region, due to long-term relationships between these emitting countries and Croatia, and because of an old tradition of tourism in this region. This explains the relatively unbroken flow of tourists emanating from these countries.

However, there was a *quasi* disappearance of other emitting countries from Western Europe such as Germany, France, the UK and the Netherlands, frightened by the media coverage of the war.

Indeed, violence, suffering, trauma, ethnic cleansing, bombings are not appreciated tourist attractions. On the contrary, violence and tourism are fundamentally incompatible, except in the case of dark tourism which will not be discussed here. Thus, war caused the leakage of customers looking for 'Sea Sun and Sand' holidays.

In addition, European governments discouraged their citizens from visiting the region, and tour operators removed the destination from their catalogues, spreading a feeling of insecurity among customers – especially Western Europe who deserted the Adriatic coastline.

The media coverage of the war in former Yugoslavia: the endangered Croatian touristic image

The mediatization of the conflict has had a devastating impact for the image of Croatia on the international stage and led to the collapse of tourism on the Croatian coast. Indeed, the media coverage of the war as a whole – not just the Croatian position – homologated the instability, barbarism, violence stereotypes characterizing the Balkans since the nineteenth century.[6]

Besides ignorance about the region, in the media a flagrant misunderstanding about this very complex war, its protagonists, its causes, its mechanisms and its nature appears: religious war, fratricidal war, interstate war, civil war? The controversies are raging among experts, journalists, humanitarians, diaspora associations, government agencies, about the responsibility of the conflict, about the identity of perpetrators of abuses and violence, about the validity of the information. Coverage of the crisis in the media takes a highly ideological dimension, and warfare of information and images is engaged in by supporters of different camps.

These rival camps accuse each other of adopting an attitude of partiality, propaganda, counter-information, in order to manipulate public opinion to its advantage.

In addition, the former Yugoslavia war's unprecedented media coverage[7] widely focused on Bosnia and was accompanied by the broadcasting of images of exceptional violence against populations, expressed in the term 'ethnic cleansing' and 'genocide', which had a tremendous impact on the international public opinion.

In turn, this instilled a sense of danger among European citizens: risk of contamination by the conflict in neighboring countries and spectre of conflagration (Legascon, 2005; Palmer, 1996) of the entire Balkan Peninsula, risk of collateral damage including accidental bombing of the Italian coast, influx of refugees, etc., which makes a region already sourcing fantasies and stereotypes even more anxiogenic.

This anxiety is exacerbated by the connection made in the media between World War II and the war in Bosnia. Pedon and Walter (1996) analyzed the photographic processing camps in Bosnia by the French media, and conclude that 'a point of view is proposed to the reader and it induces to assimilate the Serb camps of Muslim prisoners to concentration camps'[8] (p. 24).

Indeed, in the media there is a use of archetypal images that resonate in the collective memory with images of Nazi concentration camps: starved naked bodies, emaciated faces, barracks, barbed wire. These images have a symbolic value that give rise to comparison with traumatic events of world history, causing indignation of the international community. Their use enables to hide the political nature of the war, its specificities, its complexity. That leads to consider this war as a tragic repetition of history, while it is the fruit of contemporary issues.

The political dimensions of the war, its specificity, its complexity are eluded by this use of images, their symbolic content, historical parallels conducive to arouse the international community indignation, and leading to the belief that events are just a tragic repeat of history.

The media coverage of the war, the debates which it gave rise to, amalgamated and cut short, contributed to increase in the opacity of the conflict, which became hardly intelligible to the general public. These combined circumstances gave an even more disturbing image of the region.

The image of Croatia on the international scene has greatly suffered from this mediatization. This caused a major crisis in the Croatian tourism sector that tarnished the country's reputation among visitors and tour operators. Given these elements it becomes clear that the memory of the war is incompatible with the requirements of tourism industry. Given these circumstances, it is reasonable to ask how, in a country where the memory of the former Yugoslavia war occupies such a central place, tourism could recover so quickly at such a high rate?

The restoration of the Croatian touristicity[9]

Tourism is a vital sector of the Croatian economy. So the restoration of tourist flows and in particular the return of international customers was a compelling need for a country whose economy had been devastated by the conflict.

Therefore, in parallel with the reconstruction of recreational, accommodation and transportation facilities and restoration of architectural and artistic heritage damaged during the fighting, it was essential to restore the touristicity of the country to get rid of bad reputation caused by the war, to erase the remembrance of violence in minds, to attract new foreign customers and thus injecting strong foreign currency into the country's economy.

The touristicity concept developed by Théodat (2004) refers to the degree of attractiveness of a tourist destination, namely the potentiality of a territory to attract tourists. Touristicity is the result of the objective assets of the destination: its climate, culture, landscapes, tangible and intangible heritage; its accessibility: cost, distance, means of transportation; the tourist offers provided: hosting capacity, influx of tourists; type of tourism: cultural, coastal, rural, familial; transient factors such as geopolitical climate, the country's political situation, its degree of economic development, the notoriety of the destination; the absence of risk: medical, natural or political risk; and the collective imaginary linked to the destination. According to the author of this concept, the term 'touristicity' designates:

> the result of a group of physical and social factors which favor the enhancement of a territory or on the contrary lead a territory to marginality. It triggers clichés (both literally and figuratively) immediately recognizable which refer to an established code of common knowledge. These clichés are created by a selective publicity which filters the elements of a collective representation and only keeps the elements whose commercial value (which varies depending on demand) is the highest. These clichés have a decisive role in the touristic promotion. The "touristicity" of a site or a country highly depends on them. (Théodat, 2004, p. 315)[10]

The touristicity of a destination refers to the rank it occupies in a hierarchy of destinations and its place on a scale of desirability. It is largely dependent on the image that the target clientele has of the territory; thus it refers to the ability of actors to promote tourism and enhance the characteristics of the destination while standing out from the competition.

The Croatian touristicity has been undermined by the war; so it was necessary, at the end of the war, to take measures to restore the country's attractiveness. A transformation of the country's image was undertaken by stakeholders of tourism promotion in order to win back foreign visitors. In the Croatian case, the design and promotion of the tourism image devolve to the Croatian National Tourist Board. The production of this touristic image is an artificial arrangement, since it is a selection of items considered as the most profitable among a wider range of cultural, historical, material features. But this phenomenon is not the prerogative of the Croatian touristic promotion, since all tourist-receiving countries frame an image intended to attract international customers. In the next section, we will focus on the content of this promotional image.

The study of materials used in tourism promotion (website of the Croatian Tourist Board, tourist booklets emanating from the Croatian Tourist Board, catalogue and websites of tour operators) reveals that – quite logically – the war overshadowed the Croatian promotional discourse.

Indeed, tourism promoters had to create an image that corresponds with the expectations and perceptions of the target audience, while the traces of violence, inter-community resentment and suffering have no place in this spectrum.

Since the references to the violent past are inappropriate for tourists, they were erased from the tourist area and are confined to the world of *inter se*. This gives the impression that the page of war was turned, or that it never even occurred, allowing tourists to enjoy their holiday 'peacefully'.

This past, 'shameful', 'embarrassing' or 'difficult', according to Rivera (2008) is actually omitted from tourism promotion. However considering this omission as an evidence of the concealment of memory at the social level is a mistake, and we cannot consider that the memory is absent or excluded from Croatian social life, contrary to Rivera assertions:

> The CNTB's[11] decision not to recognize the war is linked to a broader absence of state-sponsored commemoration throughout the country. There are currently no national monuments or museums dedicated to the war. As of 2007, the Croatian history Museum had not expanded its collection to include exhibits pertaining to Croatia's post-independence history. [...] Moreover, despite the recommendations of international consultancies, the government has not created cultural or educational institutions dedicated either to the war or to issues of ethnic conflict. (Rivera, 2008, p. 620)

Apparently the author does not differentiate invisibility of memory in tourism promotion and complete absence of memorialization of the war, when she writes that there are no places dedicated to the war in Croatia nowadays because many examples come to invalidate this assertion. Not only are numerous monuments, memorials and museums dedicated to the patriotic war, but memorialization began precociously: first commemoration of the Oluja operation in 1996 (Pavlakovic, 2007) one year after the reconquest of the region of Knin and the end of the war, creation of the memorial-cemetery in Vukovar in 2000 (two years after the peaceful reintegration of the region), inauguration of the monument 'Wall of Pain' (in tribute to the Croatian war victims) in Zagreb in 2004, creating the HMDCDR[12] in 2004 ... therefore this difficult past has not been ostracized or repressed, it has only been concealed for foreign visitors.

Even in the coastal cities, the main destination of tourism in Croatia, expressions of the memory can be observed. However, it is generally formulated in codes which are inaccessible to foreign visitors, or visible in areas usually excluded of tourism consumption (cemeteries, modern city, etc.). Can we consider Rivera's misinterpretation of the Croatian situation as an evidence of the performativity of tourist imagery? In all instances, it raises questions (Figure 2).

The analysis of sources available to tourists and field survey data demonstrates that the reshaping of the Croatian tourism image has been articulated around two main axes: the membership of Croatia to the Mediterranean area and the novelty of the destination. This orientation widely circulates via tourism publications, foreign media and advertising campaigns abroad since the mid-2000s.

Figure 3. 'Snapshot of Croatia': 'Authenticity' (source: http://croatia.hr/fr-FR).

The enhancement of the Croatian belonging to the Mediterranean area. Tourism promotion of Croatia implies, first, to distinguish itself from the rest of the Balkan Peninsula, because it is associated with too negative connotations. Indeed, because of a lack of knowledge of the region, its culture and its history, negative representations are circulating about the Balkans, causing a sense of alterity and misunderstanding among European citizens, the main tourist clientele of Croatia.

The diversity and cultural complexity of the peninsula are muzzled by stereotypes of irrational atavistic hatreds always ready to resurface, political instability, crime and chaos (Todorova, 1997).

Hence, despite many cultural characteristics shared with its neighbors, Croatia is trying to get rid of that label considered as stigmatizing. This attempt to 'debalkanise' involves the replacement of the Balkan imagery by the Mediterranean imagery.

The data processing – from the tourist documentation – highlights invariants in self-presentation promoted by the Croatian Tourist Board.

Turquoise waters, sunshine coastline, steep and rocky coves, fishing boats, cypress and pine trees, blue sky, picturesque villages, ancient ruins, gastronomy, old town built on a the rock face, etc., all the archetypes of a Mediterranean identity, have been gathered to include Croatia in this valued cultural ensemble, making visible its Mediterranean characteristics.

Such a strategy does not generate an undeniable visual identity of the country, allowing a perfect identification of the destination (such as Venice and its gondolas, Paris and the Eiffel Tower, or Egypt and its pyramids), thanks to which it could definitely differentiate itself from the competition (French Côte d'Azur, Cyprus, Spanish Costa Brava, Crete, Malta, Italian Riviera, Sardinia, Corsica, Sicily, Greece).

On the contrary, such a campaign, through an idyllic imagery, almost caricatured aims to assert the belonging of Croatia to the Mediterranean cultural area.

The use of shared references about what makes the Mediterranean identity – in the collective imaginary – helps to anchor this claim of belonging. Thus, we find in abundance in the tourist documentation pictures of sunny peaceful streets, vines, olive trees, stone-built villages, cats basking in the sun, sailboats, Mediterranean gastronomy, elders sitting in front of colorful doors, folk costumes, etc. Because this regional affiliation is associated with the idea of sweetness of life, hospitality, authenticity, tradition and preserved heritage, advertising campaigns mobilize this privileged resource to make potential customers forget the atrocities of war.

This strategy surely helps to reassure potential tourists by the use of familiar and reassuring images. However, the promoter of tourism development is also guided by the need to stand out in a highly competitive market. Indeed, Croatia has many tourist resources (climate, landscape, cultural heritage geographical position), but it shares these assets with competing destinations and provides the same type of offer: a seasonal, seaside and family tourism. Thus, to stand out from other Mediterranean destinations, the necessity appeared to add another key message in the creation of the Croatian tourism image, because the purpose of promoters of Croatian tourism is primarily to encourage visitors to choose Croatia as a holiday resort (Figure 3).

The production of the Croatian novelty. Indeed, as Pinteau (2011) indicates in his doctoral thesis in geography dedicated to tourism in Croatia, 'The demand for this type of tourism product is saturated, due to oversupply, at least at the level of the Mediterranean'[13] (p. 136).

In line with the claim of a Mediterranean identity, the second axis of tourism policy initiated since the early 2000s consists of presenting Croatia as an original alternative to more conventional destinations. And this originality is based upon its 'novelty'. Indeed, if the Adriatic coast has never ceased to attract tourists since the nineteenth century, Croatia became an independent state only since 1991. By using a rhetorical figure, Croatia may emerge as a 'new destination', since visitors visiting this area in the past went to Yugoslavia or an Austro-Hungarian province.

Thus, the argument of the Croatian 'novelty' allows on the one hand to make forget its past by standing out of the war, and on the other hand it also allows to attract visitors weary of mass tourism, the excessive exploitation of the European littoral and the 'accumulation spaces' that are the sandy beaches.

Through the use of these representational features, Croatia is seeking to distinguish itself from saturated areas of the Mediterranean basin, where tourism is synonymous with high prices, poor-quality services, pollution, traffic jams, overcrowded beaches and folklorized culture.

Thus, this innovation would satisfy a desire for 'unusual', 'unprecedented', 'authentic' destinations. Although this 'novelty' appears to be artificial, it has been promoted in various publications (press articles, websites, documentaries) and it has especially been highlighted in the documentation design for tourist (leaflets, websites) and advertising campaigns. Promotional campaigns thus depict out-of-time landscapes, picturesque lifestyle that exude an quaint charm, conducive to relaxation and well-being.

On most of the photographs dedicated to the Croatian tourist areas (natural or urban), visitors and inhabitants are invisible, human activities are concealed and all traces of 'modernity' are hidden. This configuration conveys the impression of a 'virgin' territory, a space to be conquered by new visitors annoyed by the drawbacks of impersonal and conformist mass tourism. Thus, the 'novelty' of the destination is presented both as a pledge of tranquility and as a guarantee of a preserved local culture. Croatian tourism promotion is therefore chosen to position itself in this niche. The self-proclaimed novelty of the destination allows the country to stand out from other Mediterranean destinations, presenting itself as immune to the disadvantages suffered by the competition.

Tourism in Croatia: beyond the promoted picture

Contrary to the image promoted in media and tourist literature, Croatia is neither a new nor an exclusive touristic destination. Indeed, the Adriatic coast benefits from a tradition of tourism dating from the nineteenth century and tourist traffic features all the characteristics of mass tourism. The rise of tourism in Croatia since the mid-2000s is not an *ex nihilo* phenomenon. This is the result of previous development policies undertaken since the mid-nineteenth century which have helped to shape tourism as it is developing today.

The Yugoslav period (1945–1990)

With the defeat of Italy and the creation of the Federal People's Republic of Yugoslavia in 1945, Istria returns to the Balkan fold. The Yugoslavian coast was then mainly composed of Croatian regions of Istria and Dalmatia. From the beginning of the socialist period, considerable importance was given to the tourism sector. However, tourism development was impacted by the geopolitical context: firstly the split between Tito and Stalin (1948) led to the desertion of traditional customers from Eastern Europe (Hungary and Czechoslovakia) who disdained then Adriatic coast to turn towards the Black Sea or the Baltic Sea; and, secondly, the tourism sector had to deplore the significant decrease in arrivals from the three main emitting countries: Germany, Austria and Italy, whose economy had been deeply damaged by World War II.

This drastic drop in attendance caused a considerable loss of income, and involved an adjustment of tourism policies. Opening to the West then became essential to the financial health of the regime. So in the 1960s, measures were taken to attract the Western European customers (from France, Belgium, Great Britain, Switzerland, etc.) but also the Northern Europe customers (from Sweden, Denmark, etc.) to compensate this loss of resources by the arrival of hard currency.

Thus, the entry formalities in the country were relaxed to facilitate access for international travelers. Furthermore, a promotion policy of the destination on the international stage was implemented in order to show to customers the assets of this affordable destination.

Moreover, the Yugoslav state implemented a planning policy to encourage the development of mass tourism on the coast. This involved the creation of transport infrastructure (roads, airports), urban planning policies, creation of popular and mid-range accommodation facilities (camping, pension, vacation club and hotels – in one-, two- and three-star categories) and creation of tourism infrastructure (recreational facilities, sports facilities, malls, etc.). The development as close as possible to the shoreline was intended to offer tourists what they came to seek: the Adriatic Sea. The investments implemented by the state led to a considerable increase in hosting capacity which increased from 151,500 beds in 1960 to 860,000 in 1990.[14]

This coastal development policy, openness to Western and Northern European markets, the promotion of domestic tourism (to enable workers of the Federation to go on vacation), the return of traditional customers (Germany, Austria and Italy from the mid-1950s, then Hungary and Czechoslovakia in the 1980s) contributed to make Yugoslavia a leading tourist destination (it went from 32,000 visitors in 1948 at 5,944,000 in 1988[15]). In 1990, it ranked fourth among the top Mediterranean destinations, but the gap with the trio France–Italy–Spain was nevertheless considerable.

Yet in 1987, tourism in Yugoslavia was in crisis, due to the economic doldrums that the country was undergoing and that compromised the investments necessary for the health of the tourism sector. The inflation following the second oil shock caused a local increase in prices, coupled with an increase in air fares, making Yugoslavia less competitive and therefore less attractive to international visitors. This led to a decrease in arrivals in the late 1980s, even before the political events precipitating the fate of Croatia. However, if a reduction was already significant, the Yugoslavia war burst represents the peak of the crisis in the sector.

Present-day characteristics of tourism in Croatia

Contrary to the image induced by the promotional representation – presenting Croatia as a new destination, which implies that it would be both original and spared by the mass-tourism inconveniences – not only is tourism in Croatia the result of an ancient past (since the Austro-Hungarian period, see Pinteau about this issue), but in addition, the phenomenon presents all the characteristics of mass tourism.

This old tourist heritage, occulted in the promotional message for foreign customers, is the key factor that favored the rapid recovery of tourism after the war.

Indeed, during the previous periods of tourism development, were erected solid pillars, the destination benefits today: privileged relationship established with the major emitting countries of Europe (Germany, Austria, Italy, Hungary, Czech Republic, Slovenia) a high accommodation capacity, and efficient access means. It benefits from past planning policies and past investments, which helped enhance its coastline. It also took advantage of a strong experience in the promotion of the country and a great ability to conquer new markets, skills that were developed by tourism stakeholders in previous phases of development of the sector, and in particular during the Yugoslav period.

Thus, Croatia has inherited from its tourist past, both its infrastructure and its tourism model which characterize its current tourism attendance: strong seasonality, hypertrophy of coastal area relative to other regions, mass-tourism resort, predominantly European clientele – this population coming from central and northern Europe is mostly driven by a quest of sunshine and shoreline, that geographers have conceptualized as 'heliotropism' (Charvet, 2000) or 'désir de rivage' (Corbin, 1988; Lageiste, 2008).

Indeed, tourist flows in Croatia are mainly composed of foreign visitors (9,415,000 foreign visitors against 1.846 million domestic tourists in 2008, according to Pinteau ... quote?) and they focus quite significantly over the summer period (74% of arrivals between June and September, 49% solely during July and August). Coastal tourism accounts for 96% of overnights in 2008, making the Adriatic coast the most visited region (54 million overnights of a total of 57 million overnights were spent in the coastal regions in 2008, particularly in Istria which accounts for 51% arrivals and in Dalmatia, which accounts for 42% of arrivals). Given these factors, it can be said that tourism in Croatia is a result of mass tourism.

Croatia is not a territory uncharted for tourism. It shares the same advantages and the same disadvantages as its Mediterranean competitors, but also, currently it ranks at a 'first generation' type of development stage (characterized by mono-activity and high concentration of flows over a period and reduced space) surpassed by most Mediterranean destinations, which have attempted to diversify their offer and to develop Off-Season.

Consequently if the European travelers feel that they discovered the destination, this is evidence that large-scale marketing strategies designed to make foreign customers forget the recent past of violence and restore the country's image on the international stage have reached their goal, and are performative. Indeed, not only is it an old destination, but in addition, it has many similarities with the competition. Its success is largely due to the construction of tourism image and its large-scale promotion by tourism stakeholders, who have managed to highlight elements corresponding to latent demand (novelty seeking, authenticity, calm, etc.) even though these are an artificial arrangement.

Conclusion

As antagonistic as they may seem at first, the tourism industry and the politics of identity in Croatia are tightly interconnected. Indeed, in both cases, it matters to stand out of a Balkanic identity, because the area suffers a pejorative reputation, and it also matters to assert its singularity. Economically, this means to attract foreign customers and distinguishing itself from competitors, and politically to forge a singular national identity by differentiating itself from neighboring nations. In so doing, the tourism promotion aligns with and serves the purpose of nationalism and nation building.

Indeed, for a young state, whose sovereignty has been contested during an extremely violent war, tourism promotion can satisfy a need for distinction vis-à-vis neighboring nations and allows the country to stand out on the international scene, through the development and promotion of peculiar traditions and cultural distinctiveness, which, in turn, supports the myth of a millennia-old Croatian nation. The creation of the Croatian tourist image allows to satisfy both mercantile interests and identity claims. The attractive image of the country, reflected by promoting tourism, adds value to a fragile identity at the cost of some arrangement with past realities, including the concealment of common histories and features with the former republics of the Yugoslav Federation.

Only the relationship to war is fundamentally different in these two representations. The war is over-invested in the *inter se* circle, because of its strong cohesive virtues, but it is excluded from the tourist area due to its incompatibility with mass-tourism requirements. But if an evacuation is observed in memory of war in the tourist sphere, this does not mean that the war references are absent from the public sphere of the coastal cities, far from it. Both representations, as antagonistic they may appear, can nevertheless be geographically superimposed, because the memory of the war is expressed in an inaccessible language to foreign visitors, who do not perceive its iconography, do not grasp the meaning of its symbols and only see the destination as a new trendy 'Garden of Eden'.

Notes

1. Non-material realm of memory.

2. Author's translation. Original quote: ' Des traces parfois infinitésimales permettent d'appréhender une réalité plus profonde, qu'il serait impossible de saisir par d'autres moyens'.

3. On this issue, see Chapter 2 of the book of Paul Hockenos, *Homeland calling. Exile patriotism and the Balkan wars* (2003).

4. Author's translation. Original quote:'L'interprétation du conflit à la lumière du passé s'exprime aussi dans l'identification des acteurs du présent à ceux du passé, ce qui se traduit par l'emploi des termes četniks et ustaša non seulement par les médias au cœur du conflit et par des hommes politiques et des intellectuels, mais aussi par des gens ordinaires, et ce, encore à ce jour.[…]L'assimilation des acteurs contemporains avec ceux du passé relève de l'instrumentalisation délibérée et de la réactivation des mémoires familiales dans le contexte national. L'emploi de mêmes termes pour décrire des acteurs différents, pris dans des dynamiques diverses et dans un autre contexte, participe de l'interprétation de l'histoire selon un codage cyclique du temps (comme la répétition éternelle d'épisodes tragiques) d'autant plus facilement que les mémoires familiales encore vives des drames de la Seconde Guerre mondiale étaient prêtes à être réactivées'.

5. For example: inauguration of 'Blessed Alojzije Stepinac Museum' (in honor of the Croatian Cardinal condemned by the Partisans for his collaboration with the regime Ustasi) in 2007 in Zagreb, the presence of members of government to commemoration of the massacre of Bleiburg (Austria), including visit of the Croatian President, Kolinda Grabar-Kitarović (HDZ), during the 70th anniversary of the massacre in 2015.

6. Concerning stereotypes about the Balkans, see the book by Todorova, *Imagining the Balkans* (1997).

7. Except the precedent of the Gulf War, for which harsh criticisms were expressed on the manipulating aims of the belligerents – particularly the U.S. Army – engaged on images of war in order to influence opinion of the international public.

8. Author's translation. Original quote: ' un regard est proposé au lecteur et concours à faire assimiler les camps serbes de prisonniers musulmans à des "camps de concentration"' (p.24).

9. The analysis of the tourism promotion (message, vector, recipients) is based on a review of the tourism literature and promotional events designed for the French market. As part of this work, I have not paid attention to the tourism image intended for other markets, such as Central Europe, Northern Europe or even Germany and the UK.

10. Author's translation. Original quote: 'Le terme "touristicité" n'existe pas dans le dictionnaire; il n'a pas pour objet d'inventer un néologisme de plus, mais de cristalliser en un terme neuf et limpide un concept banal: le rang d'un site dans l'échelle de valeur des destinations de prédilection. La "touristicité" d'un territoire est la résultante d'un ensemble de facteurs physiques et sociaux qui favorisent la valorisation du séjour ou l'assignent à la marginalité. Elle se traduit par un ensemble de clichés (au propre comme au figuré) immédiatement reconnaissables, renvoyant à un code établi de connaissances communes. Ces clichés sont créés par une publicité sélective qui filtre les éléments de la représentation collective pour n'en retenir que celles dont la valeur marchande (variable selon l'offre) est la plus élevée. Ces clichés jouent un rôle décisif dans la promotion touristique. D'eux dépend en grande partie la "touristicité" d'un site ou d'un pays' (p.315).

11. Croatian National Tourism Board.

12. HRVATSKOGA MEMORIJALNO-DOKUMENTACIJSKOGA CENTRA DOMOVINSKOGA RATA:Croatian Center for Documentation and Memory of the Homeland war.

13. Author's translation. Original quote: 'la demande pour ce type de produit touristique est saturée, du fait d'une offre pléthorique, au moins à l'échelle du bassin méditerranéen' (p.136).

14. Pinteau (2011), p.340.

15. Pinteau (2011), p.319.

Disclosure statement

No potential conflict of interest was reported by the author.

References

Anderson, B. (2006). *Imagined communities: Reflection on the origin and spread of nationalism* (Revised ed.). London: Verso.

Baillie, B. (2012). *Vukovar's divided memory: The reification of ethnicity through memorialisation.* Retrieved from http://www.conflictincities.org/workingpapers.html

Banjeglav, T. (2015). *A storm of memory.* Retrieved from http://www.cultures-of-history.uni-jena.de/debating-20th-century-history/croatia/a-storm-of-memory-in-post-war-croatia/

Charvet, J.-P. (Ed.). (2000). *Dictionnaire de géographie humaine* [Dictionnary of human geography]. Paris: Liris.

Corbin, A. (1988). *Le territoire du vide. L'Occident et le désir du rivage, 1750–1840.* Paris: Aubier.

Delaperrière, M., Lory, B., & Marès, A. (Eds.). (2005). *Europe médiane. Aux sources des identités nationales* [Central Europe. At the sources of national identities]. Paris: Institut d'études slaves.

Diatkine, R. (1993). La cravate croate: narcissisme des petites différences et processus de civilisation [Croatian tie: Narcissism of small differences and civilization process]. *Revue française de psychanalyse*, tome 4, 1057–1072.

Freud, S. (1929). *Malaise dans la civilisation* [Civilization and its discontents] (2010). Paris: Payot.

Ginzburg, C. (1980). Signes, Traces, Pistes. Racines d'un paradigme indiciaire. *Le débat*, n 6, pp. 3–44. Retrieved from http://www.cairn.info/revue-le-debat-1980-6-page-3.htm

Goulding, C., & Domic, D. (2008). Heritage Identity and Ideological manipulation: The case of Croatia. *Annals of Tourism Research*, *36*, 85–102.

Hockenos, P. (2003). *Homeland calling. Exile patriotism and the Balkan wars.* Ithaca, NY: Cornell University Press.

Lageiste, J. (2008). *La plage, un objet géographique de désir* [The beach, a geographical object of desire]. Géographie et cultures. Retrieved from http://gc.revues.org/1002

Legascon, J.-S. (2005). L'europe face au défi nationaliste dans les Balkans [Europ facing nationalist challenge in the Balkans]. *Guerres mondiales et conflits contemporains*, *217*, 61–68. Retrieved from https://www.cairn.info/revue-guerres-mondiales-et-conflits-contemporains-2005-1-page-61.htm

Mac Donald, D. B. (2001). La Croatie: un exemple "d'épuration langagière"? [Croatia: An example of "linguistic cleansing"?]. *Raisons politiques*. Retrieved from http://www.cairn.info/revue-raisons-politiques-2001-2-page-127.htm

Nora, P. (1984). *Les lieux de mémoire (1997).* Paris: Gallimard.

Palmer, M. (1996). Agences de presse: urgence et concurrence [Press agencies: Emergency and competition]. *Mots*, numéro 47, 73–88. Retrieved from http://www.persee.fr/doc/mots_0243-6450_1996_num_47_1_2082

Pavlakovic, V. (2007). *Eye of the storm: The ICTY, commemorations and contested histories of Croatia's homeland war.* Retrieved from https://www.wilsoncenter.org/publication/347-eye-the-storm-the-icty-commemorations-and-contested-histories-croatias-homeland-war

Pedon, E., & Walter, J. (1996). Les variations du regard sur les « camps de concentration » en Bosnie. Analyse des usages de la photographie dans une échantillon de journaux français [Changes in perspective on the "concentration camps" in Bosnia. Analysis of the uses of photography in a sample of French newspapers]. *Mots*, 23–45.

Pinteau, F. (2011). *Le tourisme en Croatie: de la création d'une image touristique à son instrumentalisation* [Tourism in Croatia: Since the creation of a tourism image to its instrumentalization] (Unpublished doctoral dissertation). Université Clermont-Ferrand II, Clermont-Ferrand, France.

Rivera, L. (2008). Managing "Spoiled" national identity: War, tourism and memory in Croatia. *American Sociological Review*, *73*, 613–634.

Rolland-Traina, S. (2011). Mémoires ordinaires et mémoires officielles: expériences, interprétations et réécritures de l'histoire en Bosnie-Herzégovine [Ordinary and official memories: Experiences, interpretations and rewriting of history in Bosnia and Herzegovina]. *Diversité urbaine*, *10*(2), 67–89. Retrieved from http://www.erudit.org/revue/du/2011/v10/n2/1006426ar.html?vue = resume

Théodat, J.-M. (2004). L'endroit et l'envers du décor: la touristicité comparée d'Haïti et de la République dominicaine [In front and behind the scenethe compared touristicity of Haiti and the Dominican Republic]. *Tiers-mondes*, tome 45, numéro 178, 293–317.

Todorova, M. (1997). *Imaginig the Balkans*. Oxford: Oxford University Press.

Vigneault, J. (2012/4). Pour introduire la notion freudienne de narcissisme des petites différences dans l'individuel et le collectif [To introduce the Freudian notion of narcissism of small differences in the individual and collective field]. tome 4, numéro 121, *L'esprit du temps*, 37–50.

Index

For Product Safety Concerns and Information please contact our EU
representative GPSR@taylorandfrancis.com
Taylor & Francis Verlag GmbH, Kaufingerstraße 24, 80331 München, Germany